Sam Hawkins
Cross Stitch Seasons

Sam Hawkins
Cross Stitch Seasons

David & Charles

My Best Friend Shotzie
We shared
the joy of spring
the splendour of summer
the riches of autumn and
the wonders of winter
for many years,
and for all those seasons
still left for me
you will always be in my heart

A DAVID & CHARLES BOOK

First published in the UK in 2001
Designs Copyright © Sam Hawkins 2001
Photography, charts, text and layout Copyright © David & Charles 2001

Sam Hawkins has asserted his right to be identified as author of this work
in accordance with the Copyright, Designs and Patents Act, 1988.

A catalogue record for this book is available from the British Library.

ISBN 07153 1337 1

Photography by John Gollop
Styling by Susan Penny
Designed and produced by Penny & Penny
Printed in Italy by Lego
for David & Charles
Brunel House   Newton Abbot   Devon

Contents

Introduction

There is surely no more important sign of change than that of the seasons. Nature takes a new look at flora and fauna four times every year, and the weather takes a hand to change the scene completely.

It's a scientific fact that the seasons play a part in how we feel and behave – spring is the start of 'Nature's New Year' and helps us to feel more creative in our homes and gardens. That old saying 'Spring Clean' means so much more than just beating the carpets and scrubbing the floors, it is the metaphorical term for a fresh approach to life: throw out the old and welcome the new.

Stitchers the world over have always been seasonally inspired – long winter's evenings can easily be the most enjoyable time, pouring over the latest project in front of the fire, with a mug of hot chocolate and a toasted tea-cake. Up until Christmas that design may well be a cosy scene with Santa, but come January and the new year – thoughts turn to spring and a whole new palette for the needle.

In this book you will find many designs to bring that kind of pleasure: for each new season a sampler and a selection of enjoyable projects to decorate your home. At the end of each seasonal chapter is a library of extra designs for cards and keepsakes, that will take you right through the stitching year.

So, when the warmth of summer takes you out into the garden and away from your needle and thread, the imaginative designs in this book are sure to tempt you back, when nature once again sends you indoors.

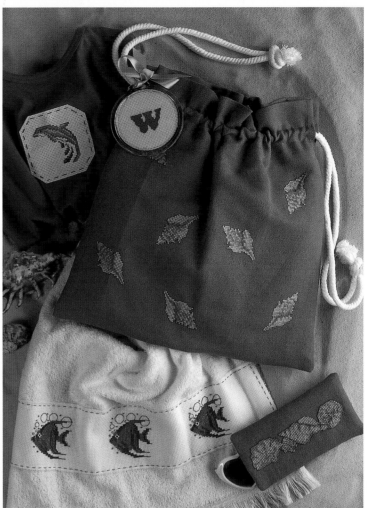

In Favour Of Birds
one must certainly
welcome
their ability to sing
as if each new spring
were the millennium

Tom Gannon

Spring Joys

Spring is a time of great activity in
the natural world: birds are building
their nests, lambs play in the fields,
and the countryside is alive with
activity after the long cold winter
months. In the lanes and woods
primroses and bluebells colour the bare
soil, and the hedgerows and trees
turn green as they open their leaves to
face the sun. The seasonal sampler in
this chapter 'In favour of birds' shows
nature at its best: birds singing as
they fly from flower to flower enjoying
the warmth of the sun while collecting
materials to build their nests. To bring
a little spring sunshine into your home,
why not stitch the café curtains, pot
holder and matching milk jug cover for
your kitchen, or the bell pull and
tie-back for your study. The fresh
colours and lively designs are sure to
lift your spirit as you enjoy the warmer,
longer days at the start of
'Nature's New Year'

'In favour of birds' is stitched on white 14 count Aida
fabric using two and three strands of stranded cotton.
The chart is on pages 18 and 19.

'In Favour of Birds' Sampler

This beautiful sampler in three panels shows a goldfinch, blue bird and chickadees playing amongst the flowers. The sampler could be personalised for an anniversary or wedding by replacing the verse in the centre panel with names and a date

- ❧ White Aida fabric, 14 count 35x42.5cm (14x17in)
- ❧ DMC stranded cotton (floss) in the colours listed in the key
- ❧ Tapestry needle, No 24
- ❧ Picture frame and mount of your choice

1 Mark the centre of your Aida fabric with tacking stitches and oversew the edges to prevent fraying. Mount the fabric in a frame or embroidery hoop.

2 Work the design from the centre out following the chart and key on pages 18 and 19. The birds, flowers and border edge are worked using three strands of stranded cotton (floss) for the cross stitch, with two strands for the flowers and leaves and one

strand on the birds. The cross stitch on the lettering in the centre panel is worked using three strands of stranded cotton (floss) with one strand for the backstitch. The remainder of the lettering is backstitched using two strands, apart from Tom Gannon which is backstitched using one strand.

Framing the sampler

1 Wash and press your stitching following the instructions on page 108. Take your work to a framer for mounting and framing, or frame it yourself following the instructions on page 108.

The detail on the birds has been backstitched using one strand of stranded cotton (floss), and the flowers and leaves backstitched in two.

Beaded Milk Jug Cover

This delightful milk jug cover is simple to stitch and will make even the plainest of jugs look exciting on the breakfast or tea table

- ❧ *White Zweigart Brittney fabric E3270, 28 count 14x14cm (5½x5½in)*
- ❧ *DMC stranded cotton (floss) in the colours listed in the key*
- ❧ *Cotton lace doily with a central area larger than 10cm (4in) diameter*
- ❧ *Selection of beads*
- ❧ *Tapestry needle, No 24*
- ❧ *White sewing thread and needle*
- ❧ *White tacking thread*

1 Mark the centre of your Brittney fabric with tacking stitches and oversew around the fabric edges to prevent fraying. Mount the fabric in a frame or embroidery hoop.

2 Work the design from the centre out following the chart and key on pages 20 and 21. Work each stitch over two threads of fabric, using two strands of stranded cotton (floss) for the cross stitch and one strand for the backstitch and french knots.

Making up the doily

1 When the design is complete wash and press it following the finishing instructions on page 108.

2 Lay your stitching on the front of the lace doily, holding it up to the light to help position the cow in the centre. Pin then tack the cow design to the doily, where the lace joins the central fabric panel. Using the tacking stitches as a guide, make a circle of close zig-zag stitches on the right side, joining the stitching to the front of the doily.

3 Working on the front of your stitching, and using sharp scissors, cut away the excess Brittney fabric just outside the circle of zig-zag stitches. Cut slowly, working right up against the stitches and taking care not to cut through the stitches or the lace edging.

4 To make sure the cover stays on the jug, the edges of the lace need to be weighted down with beads. Using a few small stitches, attach the thread to a point on the outer edge of the lace. Push the needle through a single bead or a few small beads, always ending with a seed bead. Take the needle back down through the beads starting with the second bead from the top: the top bead will act as an anchor to hold the others in place. Pull the beads up tight against the lace, then finish off with a few small stitches at the point where you started.

This cow design would make a pretty birthday greeting mounted in a circular card.

Curtain Panel

This pretty curtain has been decorated using four flower panels with a repeat border beneath.
To make the flower panels appear larger, each stitch is worked over four threads of fabric.

- ❧ *White Zweigart Brittney fabric E3270, 28 count – large enough to fit your window*
- ❧ *DMC stranded cotton (floss) in the colours listed in the key*
- ❧ *Curtain tape*
- ❧ *Tapestry needle, No 24*
- ❧ *White sewing thread and needle*
- ❧ *White tacking thread*

1 Measure your window, and cut a piece of Brittney fabric to fit the opening. Allow twice the width of your window, adding extra fabric at the top and bottom for turnings. Oversew the edges of the fabric to prevent it fraying.

2 Plan the position of the four flower panels on the fabric, making sure that they are evenly spaced across the width. You may need to repeat each panel several times, depending on the width of your window. Mark the centre point of each panel on to your fabric using tacking stitches. Plan the position of the repeat border which can go across the bottom or top of the curtain. Decide on the number of repeats you will need, and mark the centre of each on to your fabric with tacking stitches.

3 Work each panel from the centre out following the charts and key on pages 20 and 21. Work each stitch over four threads of fabric, using four strands of stranded cotton (floss) for the cross stitch, and two strands for the backstitch and french knots. Make a row of running stitches around each panel, then add a french knot to the top and bottom.

Making up the curtain

1 Wash and press your stitching following the instructions on page 109. Make your stitching into a curtain by neatening the sides, and then adding curtain tape to the top edge. Hem the bottom of the curtain so that it is the correct height for your window.

Each panel is outlined with running stitches using two strands of stranded cotton (floss), and then a french knot is added to the centre top and bottom.

Pansy Oven Mitt

This oven mitt decorated with a jug of pansies, is very quick and easy to make using a few scraps of fabric. A wooden curtain ring is sewn on to one corner of the mitt, so that it can be hung up next to your cooker

- White Aida fabric, 14 count 15x17cm (6x6in)
- DMC stranded cotton (floss) in the colours listed in the key
- Tapestry needle, No 24
- White cotton fabric – two pieces 20x20cm (8x8in)
- 100% cotton needled batting – four pieces 20x20cm (8x8in)
- White cotton bias binding – 1.1m (1¼yds)
- Wooden curtain ring 3.5cm (1⅜in) diameter
- White sewing thread and needle
- White tacking thread

1 Mark the centre of your Aida fabric with tacking stitches and oversew the edges to prevent fraying. Mount the Aida in a frame or embroidery hoop.

2 Work the design from the centre out following the chart and key on pages 20 and 21. Use two strands of stranded cotton (floss) for the cross stitch and one strand for the backstitch.

3 Wash and press your stitched Aida fabric, cotton fabric and bias binding before making up to allow for any shrinkage. Sandwich the felt between the two pieces of cotton fabric, pin then tack the layers together. Machine stitch every 2.5cm (1in) across the fabric to hold the layers together. Use sharp scissors to carefully round off three of the corners. Place the stitched Aida fabric on top of the machine stitched fabric layers, so that the top of the flower jug faces into the remaining square corner. Round off the bottom Aida corner.

4 Machine stitch a continuous length of bias binding along the bottom two edges of the Aida either side of the rounded corner.

5 Place the Aida on top of the layered fabric so that the pointed corners come together. Tack the layers together. Starting at the pointed corner, stitch bias binding around the edges, leaving a 5cm (2in) length of binding sticking out at the final corner. Fold the binding over to form a loop, and attach it securely at the back.

The padded layer on the bottom of this oven mitt will protect your hand from the heat of the oven.

Wishing Well Bell-pull

This pretty design of a wishing well is small enough to be made into a greetings card, but when each stitch is worked over two threads of Lincoln fabric it can also be made into a decorative bell-pull

- White Zweigart Lincoln fabric E3327, 14 count 41x21.5cm (16x8½in)
- DMC stranded cotton (floss) in the colours listed in the key
- Tapestry needle, No 24
- White cotton fabric, 41x21.5cm (16x8½in)
- 100% cotton needled batting 35.5x16.5cm (14x6½in)
- White plastic curtain rings – two 3.5cm (1⅜in) diameter
- Piping cord 1.1m (1¼yds)
- Length of pajama cord
- White sewing thread and needle
- White tacking thread

1 Mark the centre of your Lincoln fabric with tacking stitches and oversew the edges to prevent fraying. Mount the fabric in a frame or embroidery hoop before you start.

2 Work the design from the centre out following the chart and key on pages 22 and 23. Use four strands of stranded cotton (floss) for the cross stitch and two strand for the backstitch and french knots, working each stitch over two threads of fabric.

3 Wash and press the design following the instructions on page 108. Working on the right side of the fabric, measure 1cm (⅜in) outside the last row of stitching and make a row of tacking stitches around all four sides – this will be the final size of your bell-pull. If you would like a larger bell-pull then leave a wider border of fabric around your stitching.

4 Lay the batting on a flat surface, on top of this place the backing fabric right side up, and then the stitched design right side facing down. Using the tacking stitches on the stitched fabric as a guide, tack then sew around the edges of the bell-pull through all three layers of fabric. Leave a small gap on one long side for turning.

5 Using sharp scissors trim away the excess fabric leaving a seam allowance of about 4mm (⅛in). Clip the corners of the bell-pull by making small cuts in the seam allowance, from the edge of the fabric halfway to the seam. Turn the bell-pull to the right side through the gap left in the stitching.

6 Push one end of the piping cord into the gap on the side of the bell-pull. Using a needle threaded with cotton the same colour as the piping cord make a few stitches on the inside of the bell-pull to secure the cord end. Attach the cord around the edges of the bell-pull using small neat stitches. When you have returned to the point where you started, push the cord end into the gap and secure it with a few stitches. Sew up the gap making sure the cord ends are hidden inside.

7 Sew a large plastic curtain ring on to the centre back of the bell-pull at the top and bottom. Attach a ready-made tassel to the bottom ring or make your own with a length of thick piping or pajama cord. Fold the cord in half, loop it through the bottom ring and then tie a knot to hold it in place. Unravel the cut ends of the cord to make a tassel.

Floral Tie-back

Brighten plain curtains with this pretty floral tie-back. Stitched to match the tie-back on page 15, it will be a reminder of warm spring days when it's cold outside

- *White Zweigart Lincoln fabric E3327, 14 count 18×70cm (7×28in)*
- *DMC stranded cotton (floss) in the colours listed in the key*
- *Tapestry needle, No 24*
- *White cotton fabric, 18×70cm (7×28in)*
- *100% cotton needled batting 18×70cm (7×28in)*
- *White plastic curtain rings – two 3.5cm (1³/₈) in diameter*
- *Piping cord 1.40m (1¹/₂yds)*
- *White sewing thread and needle*
- *White tacking thread*

1 Fold the Lincoln fabric in half to find the centre. Mark this point with tacking stitches then oversew the edges to prevent fraying. The centre point on the fabric is marked on the chart with an arrow, this is not the centre of the design but the point where the stitching should begin. The chart is printed so that when stitched it will make a tie-back to go on the right side of your window. If you want to make a left tie-back or you want to stitch on both sides, then the chart will have to be reversed. Mount the section of the fabric that you will be stitching into a frame.

Start stitching at the point on the fabric and the chart marked with an arrow. The dotted line is the stitching line along the top and bottom edge of the fabric.

2 Work the design from the arrow marked on the chart on page 22, at the point marked on the fabric with a tacking stitch. Use four strands of stranded cotton (floss) for the cross stitch and two strands for the backstitch and french knots, working each stitch over two threads of fabric. If you want to stitch on the other side of your tie-back, work the design again, on the other end of the fabric. Wash and press the stitching following the instructions on page 108.

3 Working on the right side of the stitching, make a row of tacking stitches 1cm (³/₈in) above the design, keeping the same distance away from the stitching. Repeat along the bottom edge – this will be the shape of your tie-back (see diagram).

4 Stitch the design, backing fabric and batting together along the top and bottom edges, in the same way as for the tie-back, but leaving the ends open. Trim away the excess fabric, and turn the tie-back to the right side.

5 Sew piping cord along the top and bottom edges of the tie-back. Thread a plastic curtain ring on to one end of the tie-back. Fold over the fabric and secure it on the reverse side with small neat stitches. Repeat for the other end.

Spring Sampler

DMC stranded cotton (floss)

⊡	Blanc	⧉	818
◲	208	▨	825
△	211	I	827
■	310	◔	890
↑	318	◣	919
→	319	↓	922
⊕	326	6	3326
◁	335	Y	3813
∩	351	◳	3815
◁	367	▥	3818
▽	368	**Backstitch**	
◪	413	◿	310
▤	414	◿	318
✕	433	◿	319
◇	434	◿	326
4	436	◿	414
⊠	445	◿	436
▨	550	◿	550
✳	601	◿	601
⅄	603	◿	610
⊓	605	◿	725
◔	610	◻	762
⊳	612	◿	798
⫽	701	◿	823
⌣	703	◿	825
◻	721	◹	827
✓	725	◿	838
←	738	◿	890
⋁	745	◿	919
⁒	762	◿	3818
◓	797	**French knots**	
+	798	⬤	838
−	799		
Ⅴ	801		
✦	809		
⊠	813		

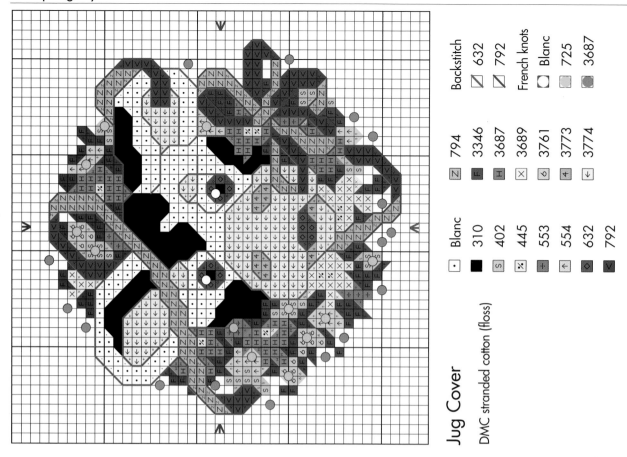

Jug Cover

DMC stranded cotton (floss)

·	Blanc	
■	310	
S	402	
%	445	
+	553	
←	554	
◇	632	
V	792	

Z	794	
F	3346	
H	3687	
×	3689	
◊	3761	
4	3773	
↓	3774	

Backstitch
╱	632
╱	792

French knots
○	Blanc
○	725
●	3687

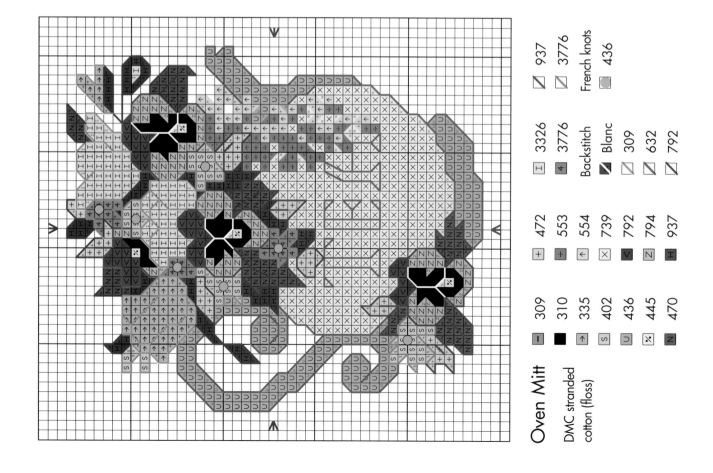

Oven Mitt

DMC stranded
cotton (floss)

I	309	
■	310	
↑	335	
S	402	
U	436	
%	445	
N	470	

+	472	
✦	553	
←	554	
×	739	
V	792	
Z	794	
H	937	

I	3326	
4	3776	

Backstitch
◢	Blanc
╱	309
╱	632
╱	792

╱	937
╱	3776

French knots
●	436

Curtain Panel

DMC stranded cotton (floss)

· Blanc	T 783	⊿ 898
◼ 319	Z 818	⊿ 3346
↑ 335	F 828	French knots
N 368	◼ 898	◼ 898
/ 369	I 3326	
◼ 550	◼ 3346	
U 552	▷ 3347	
= 553	S 3348	
← 554	+ 3773	
/ 725	↓ 3774	
V 727	Backstitch	
X 739	⊿ 550	

Bell-pull

DMC stranded cotton (floss)

■	319		Backstitch
◉	367	⊘	319
⊞	434	⊘	434
▷	436	⊘	553
N	553	⊘	646
‖	554	⊘	722
⋒	646	⊘	725
⊣	648	⊘	798
✕	722	⊘	801
↑	725	⊘	839
=	727	⊘	3345
✚	798	⊘	3347
U	800	⊘	3688
◣	801		French knots
I	839	●	319
Z	841	●	434
H	842	●	553
←	3072	●	798
■	3345	●	3688
◀	3347		
✕	3348		
▽	3688		
S	3689		

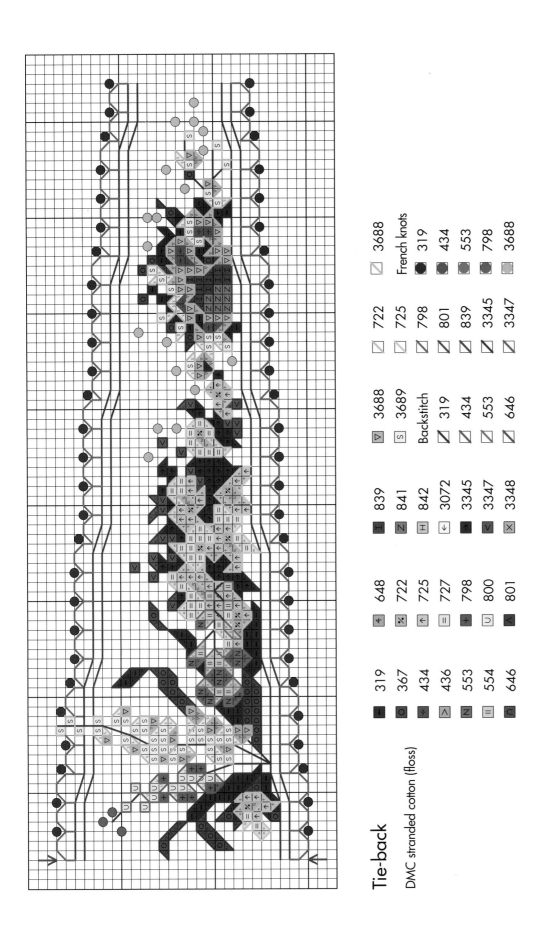

Tie-back

DMC stranded cotton (floss)

▮	319	✦	648	▮	839	▷	3688	▱	3688
○	367	✕	722	N	841	S	3689		French knots
+	434	←	725	H	842		Backstitch	●	319
⋀	436	=	727	↓	3072	▱	319	●	434
N	553	+	798	▲	3345	▱	434	●	553
=	554	∪	800	V	3347	▱	553	●	798
∪	646	◥	801	✕	3348	▱	646	●	3688
						▱	722		
						▱	725		
						▱	798		
						▱	801		
						▱	839		
						▱	3345		
						▱	3347		

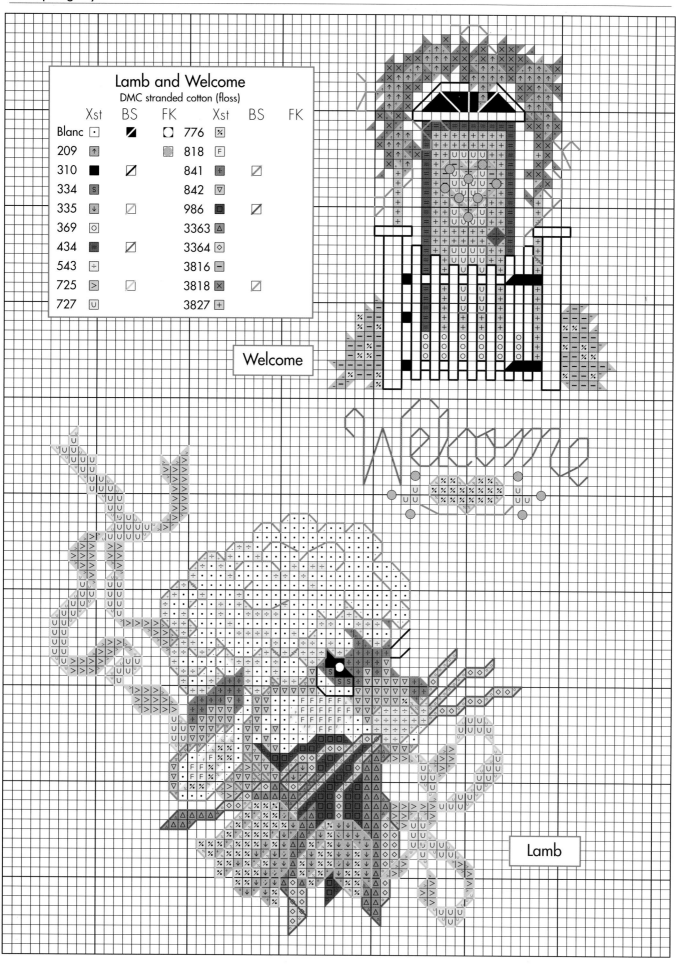

Lamb and Welcome
DMC stranded cotton (floss)

	Xst	BS	FK		Xst	BS	FK
Blanc	·	◪	◖	776	%		
209	↑			818	F		
310	■	◿		841	+	◿	
334	S			842	▽		
335	↓	◿		986	■	◿	
369	○			3363	△		
434	▦	◿		3364	◇		
543	÷			3816	−		
725	▷	◿		3818	✕	◿	
727	U			3827	+		

Welcome

Lamb

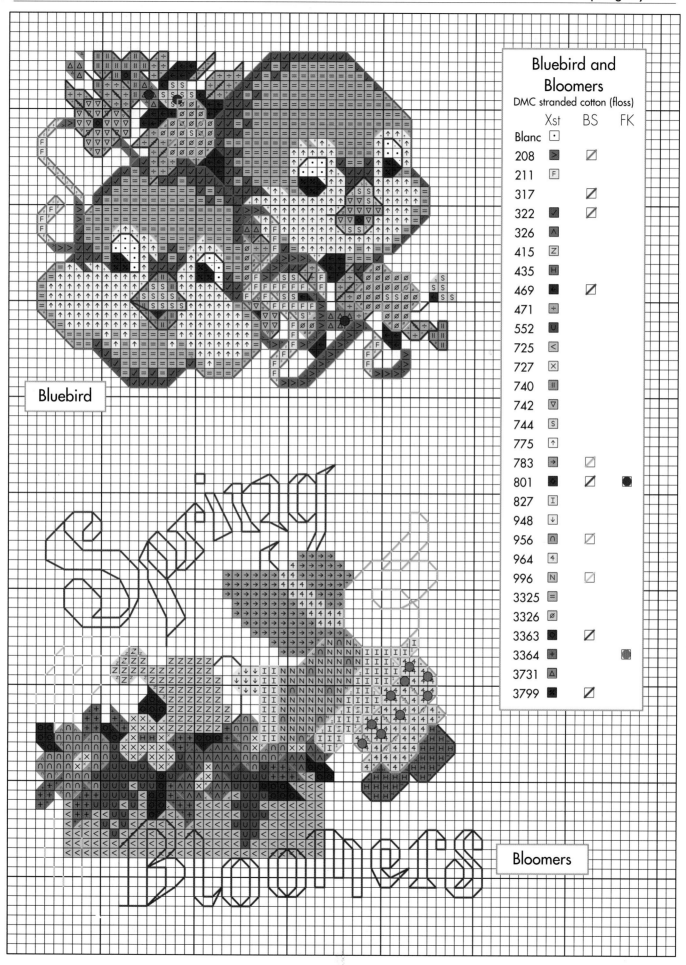

Bluebird

Bloomers

	Xst	BS	FK
Blanc	·		
208	▶	╱	
211	F		
317		╱	
322	✓	╱	
326	△		
415	Z		
435	H		
469	◼	╱	
471	÷		
552	U		
725	<		
727	✕		
740	‖		
742	▽		
744	S		
775	↑		
783	→	╱	
801	◈	╱	●
827	I		
948	↓		
956	∩	╱	
964	4		
996	N	╱	
3325	=		
3326	∅		
3363	◉	╱	
3364	+		◼
3731	△		
3799	▨	╱	

Bluebird and Bloomers

DMC stranded cotton (floss)

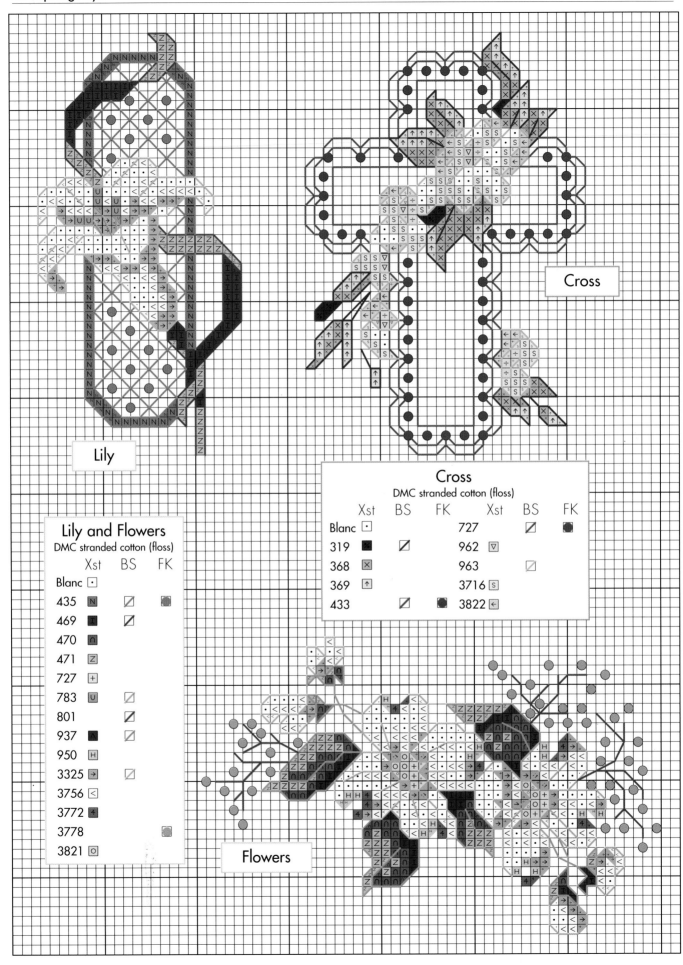

Cross

Lily

Lily and Flowers
DMC stranded cotton (floss)

	Xst	BS	FK
Blanc	·		
435	N	◿	●
469	I	◿	
470	∩		
471	Z		
727	+		
783	U	◿	
801		◿	
937	■	◿	
950	H		
3325	→	◿	
3756	<		
3772	◢		
3778			▧
3821	○		

Cross
DMC stranded cotton (floss)

	Xst	BS	FK		Xst	BS	FK
Blanc	·			727	◿		●
319	■	◿		962	▽		
368	⊠			963		◿	
369	↑			3716	S		
433		◿	●	3822	←		

Flowers

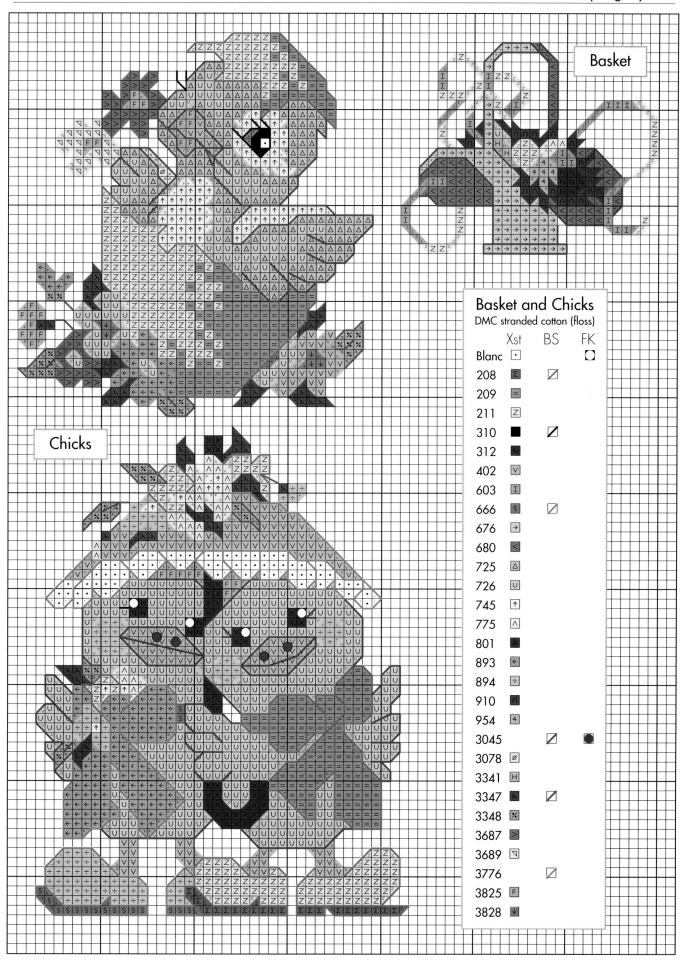

Basket

Chicks

Basket and Chicks
DMC stranded cotton (floss)

	Xst	BS	FK
Blanc	·		◌
208	Σ	╱	
209	=		
211	Z		
310	■	╱	
312	N		
402	V		
603	I		
666	S	╱	
676	→		
680	◄		
725	△		
726	U		
745	↑		
775	∧		
801	■		
893	←		
894	÷		
910	■		
954	4		
3045		╱	●
3078	∅		
3341	H		
3347	■	╱	
3348	╳		
3687	>		
3689	◩		
3776		╱	
3825	F		
3828	↓		

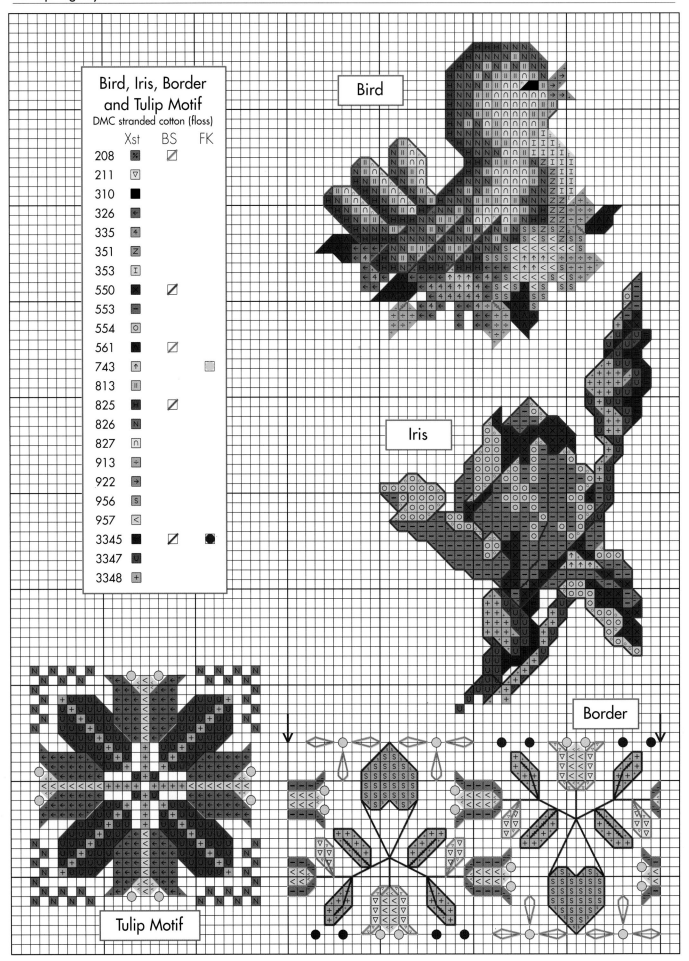

Bird, Iris, Border and Tulip Motif

DMC stranded cotton (floss)

	Xst	BS	FK
208	▨	◪	
211	▽		
310	■		
326	◄		
335	◢		
351	☑		
353	I		
550	✕	◪	
553	–		
554	○		
561	■	◪	
743	↑		▢
813	II		
825	⊢	◪	
826	N		
827	∩		
913	±		
922	→		
956	S		
957	<		
3345	■	◪	●
3347	U		
3348	+		

Bird

Iris

Border

Tulip Motif

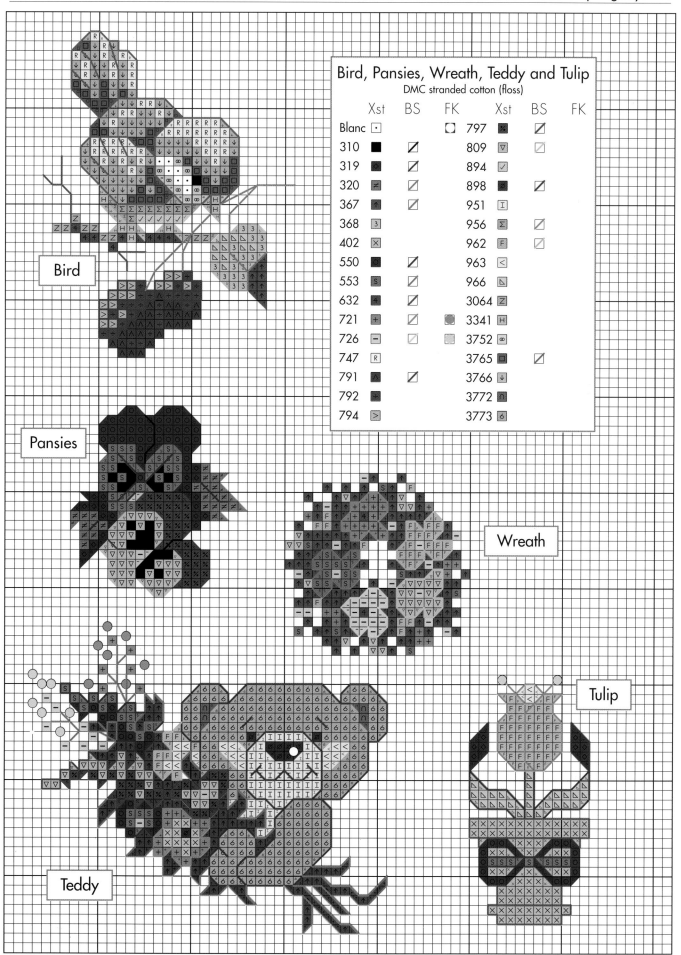

Bird, Pansies, Wreath, Teddy and Tulip
DMC stranded cotton (floss)

	Xst	BS	FK		Xst	BS	FK
Blanc	·		◯	797	▨	◨	
310	■	◨		809	▽	◨	
319	◧	◨		894	✓		
320	⊄	◨		898	◙	◨	
367	↑	◨		951	I		
368	3			956	Σ	◨	
402	✕			962	F	◨	
550	▣	◨		963	<		
553	S	◨		966	∟		
632	4	◨		3064	Z		
721	+	◨	●	3341	H		
726	−	◨	◉	3752	∞		
747	R			3765	▢	◨	
791	▲	◨		3766	↓		
792	⊟			3772	∩		
794	▷			3773	6		

Bird

Pansies

Wreath

Tulip

Teddy

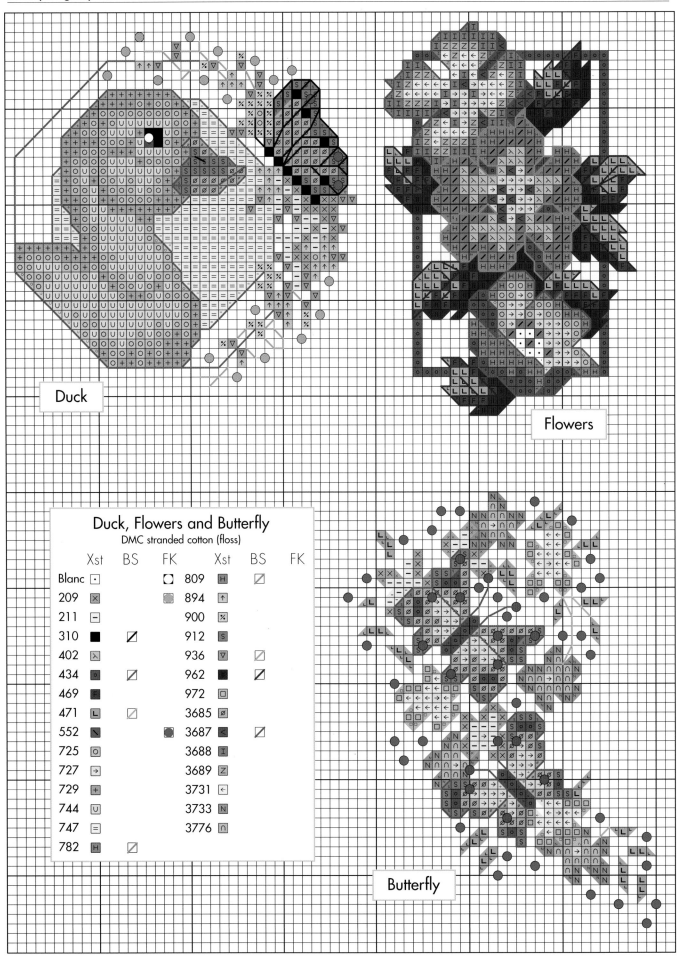

Duck

Flowers

Butterfly

Duck, Flowers and Butterfly
DMC stranded cotton (floss)

	Xst	BS	FK		Xst	BS	FK
Blanc	·			809	H		
209	⊠			894	↑		
211	−			900	⊠		
310	■	╱		912	S		
402	⊠			936	▽		╱
434	◙	╱		962	■		╱
469	⊞			972	▫		
471	L	╱		3685	⊘		
552	◪		●	3687	◤		╱
725	○			3688	I		
727	→			3689	Z		
729	+			3731	←		
744	U			3733	N		
747	=			3776	∩		
782	H	╱					

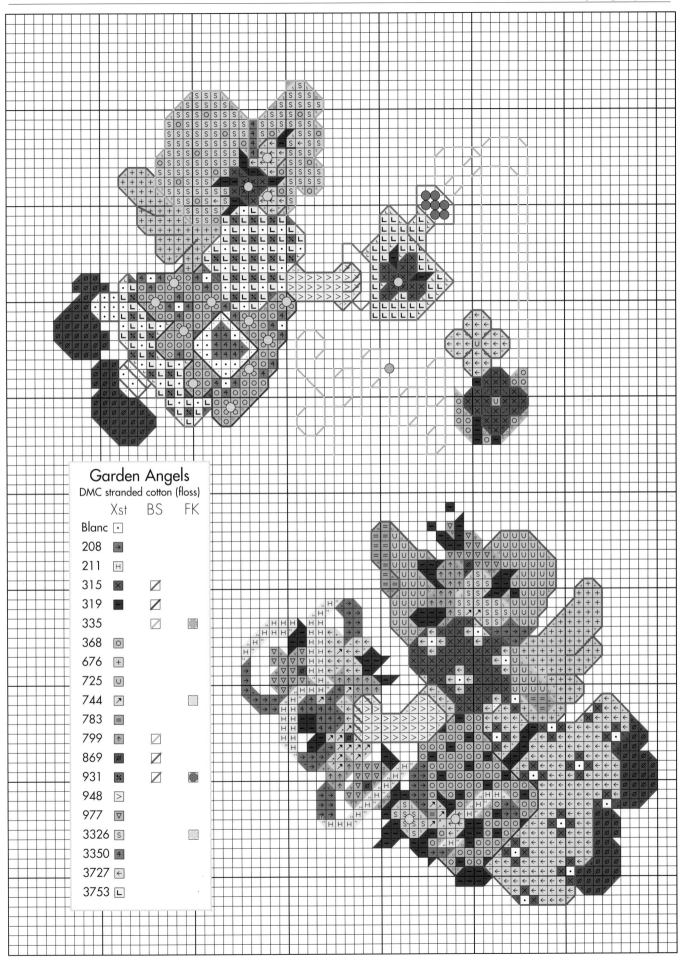

Garden Angels
DMC stranded cotton (floss)

	Xst	BS	FK
Blanc	·		
208	→		
211	H		
315	✕	╱	
319	■	╱	
335		╱	▣
368	○		
676	+		
725	U		
744	↗		▢
783	=		
799	↑	╱	
869	▨	╱	
931	％	╱	▣
948	>		
977	▽		
3326	S		▨
3350	4		
3727	←		
3753	L		

I have a garden of my own,
But so with roses overgrown,
And lilies, that you would't guess
to be a little wilderness.

Andrew Marvell

Summer's Splendour

Summer is a time of great enjoyment: gardens are alive with colour, the smell of newly mown grass fills the air, and we all enjoy a trip to the seaside or a picnic in the country. The sampler in this chapter shows the beauty of a summer garden: roses and peonies are in full bloom, opening their petals to bask in the warmth of the summer sun. For outings to the beach, the shell bag and sunglasses case will keep all your belongings in a safe place; or use the bag and the fish towel to give your bathroom a seaside theme. For special picnics or entertaining in the garden why not stitch the cutlery bag, napkin and matching tray, which are decorated with everybody's favourite summer fruit, the strawberry. When summer is over, these projects will remind you of warm, happy days spent in the garden or at the beach

'Summer's Splendour' is stitched on white 14 count Aida fabric using one and two strands of stranded cotton. The chart is on pages 42 and 43.

Summer Garden Sampler

This pretty sampler featuring a poem by Andrew Marvell, is a glorious tribute to the summer garden and the beauty of nature

- ❧ *White Aida fabric, 14 count 35x42.5cm (14x17in)*
- ❧ *DMC stranded cotton (floss) in the colours listed in the key*
- ❧ *Tapestry needle, No 24*
- ❧ *Picture frame and mount of your choice*

1 Mark the centre of your Aida fabric with tacking stitches and oversew the edges to prevent fraying. Mount the fabric in a frame or embroidery hoop.

2 Work the design from the centre out following the chart and key on pages 42 and 43. The border, flowers, ribbon and capital letters of the poem are worked in cross stitch using two strands of stranded cotton (floss), and the backstitch and french knots in one strand.

Framing the sampler

1 Wash and press your stitching following the instructions on page 108. Take your work to a framer for mounting and framing, or frame it yourself following the instructions on page 108.

The realistic looking flowers on this sampler have been created using subtle shading, and dark brown backstitch to outline each petal.

Shell Beach Bag

This useful bag featuring a single shell motif is a great way to take your belongings to the beach. It can also be used as a sponge bag by lining it with waterproof fabric

- *Wedgewood blue Zweigart Quaker Cloth , 28 count – two pieces 40x35cm (16x14in)*
- *DMC stranded cotton (floss) in the colours listed in the key*
- *White cotton – two pieces 29x35cm (11x14in)*
- *Thick piping cord or pajama cord – two pieces each 0.9m (1yd)*
- *Tapestry needle, No 24*
- *White and blue sewing thread and needle*
- *White tacking thread*

1 Mark the centre of one piece of Quaker Cloth with tacking stitches and oversew around the fabric edges to prevent fraying. Mount the fabric in a frame or embroidery hoop.

2 Work the shell motif randomly over the fabric, turning the fabric as you work each shell, and following the chart and key on pages 44 and 45. Use three strands of stranded cotton (floss) for the cross stitch and two strands for the backstitch, working each stitch over two threads of fabric.

Making the bag

1 Place the two pieces of Quaker Cloth together, with the stitching facing inward – the two longer edges are the sides of the bag. Using a 1cm (3/8in) seam allowance sew across the bottom and up both sides of the bag, leaving 11cm (4¼in) open at the top on both sides. Turn the bag through to the right side. Working at the top on one side of the bag, turn over the seam allowance once, on the front of the bag between the top of the side seam and the top of the

fabric. Catch stitch it in place. Repeat for the back then do the same for the other side of the bag.

With right sides of the fabric together sew down the sides and across the bottom to make a bag. Neaten the seam allowance on the side seams at the top of the bag.

2 Turn down 7cm (2¾in) at the top of the bag on both the front and back edges. Tack the turnings in place inside the bag.

3 Working on the right side of the bag, machine stitch across both the front and back sides of the bag 3cm (1¼in) down from the top folded edge. Make another row of machine stitches 2cm (¾in) down from the first row. Finally stitch a third row right

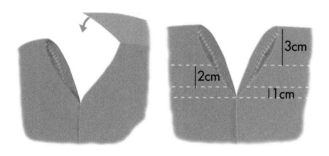

Turn over the top 7cm (2¾in) of the bag. Machine stitch around the bag to make channels for the cord.

around the bag at the point where the side seam and the side opening meet.

4 Place the two pieces of lining fabric together. Sew down the two short sides and across the bottom to make a bag. With the lining bag still on the wrong side, turn over the top edge 1cm (⅜in) on to the wrong side. Iron the turning in place. Push the lining inside the bag, so that the bottom row of machine stitches is level with the folded top edge of the lining. Tack then catch stitch the lining to the bag.

5 Thread a length of cord through the top machine channel on the front of the bag, repeat for the back. Tie the cords together at either end with a knot.

Shell Sunglasses Case

This useful case stitched with a shell design and padded with batting, is a handy place to keep your sunglasses when they are not in use

- *Wedgewood blue Zweigart Quaker Cloth, 28 count – two pieces 17x10cm (6¾x4in)*
- *DMC stranded cotton (floss) in the colours listed in the key*
- *White cotton fabric – two pieces 17x10cm (6¾x4in)*
- *100% cotton batting – two pieces 17x10cm (6¾x4in)*
- *Tapestry needle, No 24*
- *White and blue sewing thread and needle*

1 Mark the centre of one piece of Quaker Cloth with tacking stitches, oversew the edges and mount in an embroidery hoop. Work the shell design on the fabric, following the chart and key on pages 44 and 45. Use three strands of stranded cotton (floss)

for the cross stitch and two strands for the backstitch, working each stitch over two threads of fabric.

2 Sandwich the stitching between the batting and the lining, with the right sides of the stitching and lining facing. Stitch along one short edge making a 1cm (⅜in) seam allowance. Repeat with the other pieces of Quaker Cloth and lining.

3 Open out one piece of joined fabric, iron the seam flat. Repeat for the second, then place the pieces right sides together on the table. Sew around the outer edge with a 1cm (⅜in) seam allowance, leaving a small gap for turning. Turn the case to the right side through the gap in the seam. Sew up the gap with small stitches, then push the lining inside the case.

Beach Towel, Dolphin Motif and Tag

Fish and a dolphin have been used to decorate this pretty towel and t-shirt. The designs which can be found on pages 44 and 45 could also be used to make greetings cards

- White Aida fabric, 14 count 10cm (4in) x the width of your towel; 8.5x8.5cm (3¼x3¼in) for the dolphin; a 7.5cm (3in) approximate circle for the tag
- DMC stranded cotton (floss) in the colours listed in the key
- Tapestry needle, No 24
- White towel
- Clear luggage tag 7.3cm (3in) diameter
- Iron-on vilene – the same size as the fabric
- Sewing needle and thread
- Bondaweb

Making the fish towel edging

1 Cut a length of Aida fabric the width of your towel adding 2.5cm (1in) to the ends for neatening. Work out how many fish repeats you will be stitching – they can be any distance apart, as long as they are evenly spaced. Mark the centre point of each fish with a tacking stitch and oversew the edges of the

Aida to prevent it fraying. Work each fish from the centre out, using two strands of stranded cotton (floss) for the cross stitch, and one for the backstitch and french knots.

2 Cut the stitched Aida panel down to 7.5cm (3in), and the width of your towel. Apply a length of iron-on vilene to the back of the panel. Machine stitch around the edges of the panel using a tight zig-zag.

3 Using two strands of stranded cotton (floss) make a row of running stitches around the panel, one square inside the zig-zag stitching, using the same thread colour used for the bubbles. Machine stitch the panel on to the towel just inside the zig-zag stitching.

Making the t-shirt motif

1 Stitch the dolphin design on to the fabric, using two strands for the cross stitch and one for the backstitch. Iron bondaweb on to the back of the design. Cut off the corners of the fabric, then make a row of running stitching around the edge. Peel off the backing fabric from the design, lay it on the front of the t-shirt and iron in place.

Making the tag

1 Using the chart and key on page 44 and 45, stitch your chosen initial in the centre of your Aida fabric, using two strands for the cross stitch and one to outline the letter. Iron vilene on to the back of your design, then using the template provided with the tag, cut the fabric to size. Place the stitched fabric in the tag and snap on the back.

Strawberry Cutlery Bag

This pretty strawberry bag, lined with green gingham fabric, can be used to keep cutlery or napkins. By making the bag longer it could also be used for storing a baguette

- ❦ *White Jobelan fabric, 28 count 34x21cm (13³⁄₄x8¹⁄₂in)*
- ❦ *Green cotton gingham fabric 34x21cm (13³⁄₄x8¹⁄₂in)*
- ❦ *DMC stranded cotton (floss) in the colours listed in the key*
- ❦ *Pink 6mm (¹⁄₄in) satin ribbon*
- ❦ *Tapestry needle, No 24*
- ❦ *Sewing needle and thread*

1 Cut the Jobelan fabric in half so that you have two rectangles 17x21cm (6³⁄₄x8¹⁄₂in). Cut the gingham fabric in half in the same way. On one rectangle of Jobelan oversew the edges, and make a tacking stitch 7cm (2³⁄₄in) from one short edge, and halfway between the long edges.

2 Start stitching from the centre of the design at the point on the fabric marked with a tacking stitch. Use three strands of stranded cotton (floss) for the cross

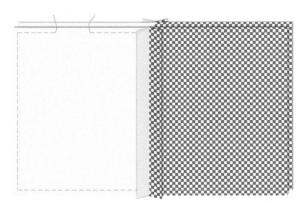

Join one piece of Jobelan fabric to a piece of gingham. Repeat with the other two pieces of fabric. With right sides facing sew around the outer edge, leaving a small gap for turning.

stitch, two strands for the green backstitched tendrils and the lettering, and one for the butterfly, leaf and flower markings, working each stitch over two threads of fabric. The french knots are worked in one strand for the strawberries, and two for the butterfly antennas.

3 With right sides together, stitch one piece of gingham to the stitched design along the short edge furthest away from the cross stitch, with a 1cm (³⁄₈in) seam allowance. Repeat with the other pieces of Jobelan and gingham fabric. Open out one piece of joined fabric, iron the seam flat and lay it right side up on the table. Repeat for the second piece and lay it right side down on top of the first. Join the pieces together by sewing around the outer edge with a 1cm (³⁄₈in) seam allowance, leaving a gap for turning.

4 Turn the bag to the right side, through the hole left in the outer seam. Sew up the hole then push the lining down inside the bag. Place napkins or cutlery in the bag and secure the top with a length of ribbon.

Strawberry Napkin

The triangular strawberry design can be stitched around the edge of the napkin, or you could make a tablecloth repeating the motif four times in the centre to form a square, and then again around the edges of the cloth

- ❧ *White Jobelan fabric, 28 count 41x41cm (16x16in)*
- ❧ *DMC stranded cotton (floss) in the colours listed in the key*
- ❧ *Tapestry needle, No 24*
- ❧ *Sewing needle and thread*

1 Turn over one edge of the fabric by 6mm (¼in), and then again by another 6mm (¼in). Repeat for the other three sides. Tack then stitch around the napkin to neaten the edges.

2 Stitch the triangular shaped strawberry design on page 46 and 47, on the edge of one side of the napkin, so that the design is just inside the turning on the edge of the fabric. Use three strands of stranded cotton (floss) for the cross stitch, two strands for the green backstitched tendrils and one for the butterfly, leaf and flower markings, working each stitch over two threads of fabric. The french knots are worked in one strand for the strawberries, and two for the butterfly antennas. The design can be repeated on all four edges of the napkin.

Strawberry Tray

This attractive tray is a great way to serve cream tea on a summer's afternoon. The dark wood tray has been painted with white emulsion, dragged with strawberry coloured paint, and then coated with clear varnish

- ❧ *White Jobelan fabric, 28 count 30x20cm (12x8in)*
- ❧ *DMC stranded cotton (floss) in the colours listed in the key*
- ❧ *Tapestry needle, No 24*
- ❧ *Sudberry House tray – WTT*

1 Mark the centre of your fabric, then oversew the edges before mounting it in a frame or embroidery hoop. Work the design from the centre out following the chart and key on pages 46 and 47.

Only the bottom half of the design is shown on the chart, to stitch the design again, turn the fabric upside down. Stitch the design in the same way as for the napkin or bag, working each stitch over two threads.

2 Mount the fabric on the backboard supplied with the tray. Position the stitching behind the glass, and then insert the backboard and baize backing.

The strawberry tray and napkin designs could easily be adapted for a tablecloth centrepiece.

Summer Sampler

DMC stranded cotton (floss)

·	Blanc	Backstitch	
V	209	⟋	986
↓	211	⟋	801
+	335	French knots	
Σ	402	░	727
✕	434	●	801
◇	727	▨	3776
▽	744		
‰	745		
∅	754		
≠	775		
<	782		
−	818		
N	826		
H	827		
↑	945		
△	948		
=	951		
◄	986		
4	988		
‖	989		
○	3326		
►	3346		
✤	3347		
∧	3348		
Z	3753		
F	3756		
U	3770		
I	3776		
S	3820		

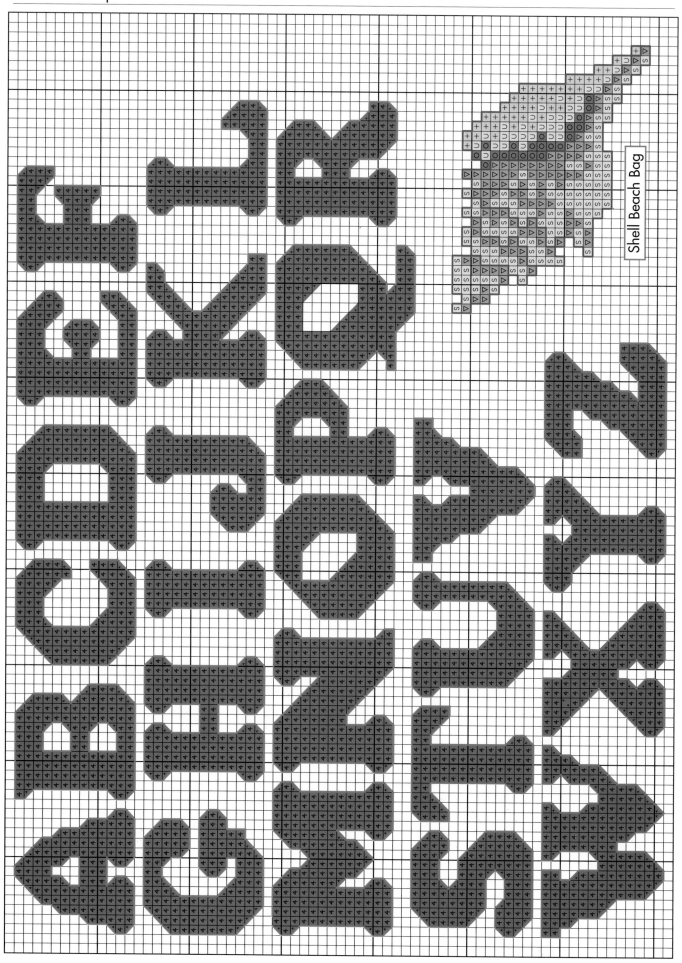

Shell Beach Bag

Beach Set

DMC stranded cotton (floss)

·	Blanc	
+	210	
■	310	
○	553	
◆	699	
◇	702	
‖	798	
←	799	
✕	800	
∪	957	
▷	3778	
s	3779	

Backstitch

╱	699
╱	798
╱	995
╱	3777

French knots

▨	995

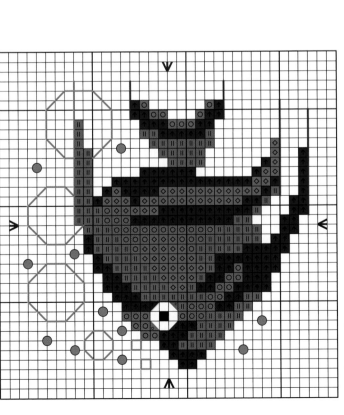

Beach Towel

Dolphin Motif

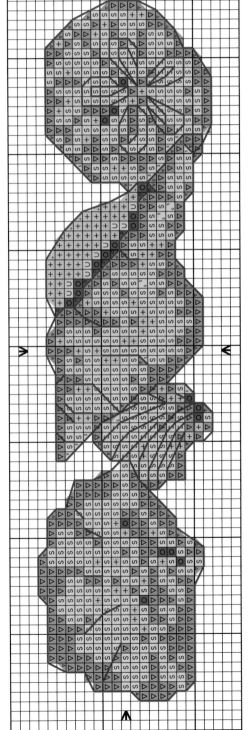

Shell Sunglasses Case

Tray

Picnic Set

DMC stranded
cotton (floss)

Symbol	Color
⊡	Blanc
⊞	300
⊠	301
I	402
▦	498
⊙	702
S	704
▽	743
＼	745
✕	891
U	894
↑	910
→	3689

Backstitch

Symbol	Color
╱	300
╱	498
╱	891
╱	910

French knots

Symbol	Color
●	300
●	498
●	743

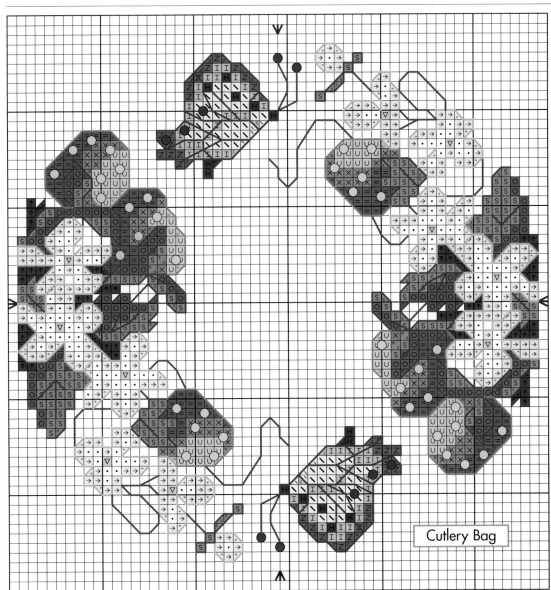

Cutlery Bag

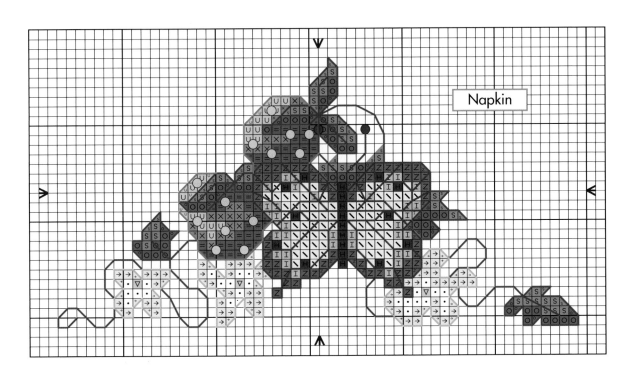

Napkin

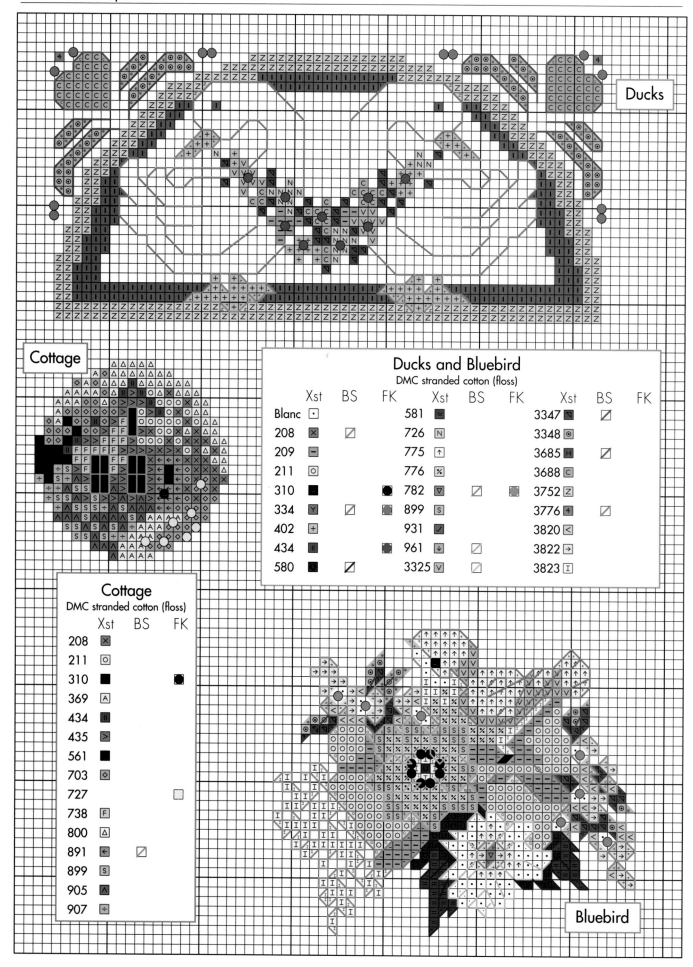

Ducks

Cottage

Ducks and Bluebird
DMC stranded cotton (floss)

	Xst	BS	FK		Xst	BS	FK		Xst	BS	FK
Blanc	·			581	▬			3347	◩	◪	
208	✕	◪		726	N			3348	◉		
209	▬			775	↑			3685	H	◪	
211	◎			776	⅔			3688	C		
310	■		●	782	▽	◪	▣	3752	Z		
334	Y	◪	▣	899	S			3776	◧	◪	
402	✛			931	◪			3820	◁		
434	‖		▣	961	↓	◪		3822	→		
580	■	◪		3325	∨	◪		3823	I		

Cottage
DMC stranded cotton (floss)

	Xst	BS	FK
208	✕		
211	◎		
310	■		▣
369	A		
434	‖		
435	▷		
561	■		
703	◈		
727			▢
738	F		
800	◬		
891	←	◪	
899	S		
905	◪		
907	✛		

Bluebird

Melon

Bird

Summertime

Melon, Bird and Summertime
DMC stranded cotton (floss)

	Xst	BS	FK
Blanc	⊡		
310	■	◿	
321	I		
435	‖		
436	Σ		
470	O		
472	−		
552		◿	
553	S		
702	↑		
704	∩		
738	⟋		
815	U		
840	3		
841	←		
890	Z		
892	4		
907	∧	◿	
911		◿	
930	⊠	◿	
986	■	◿	
988	F		
3345	■		
3753	⊠		

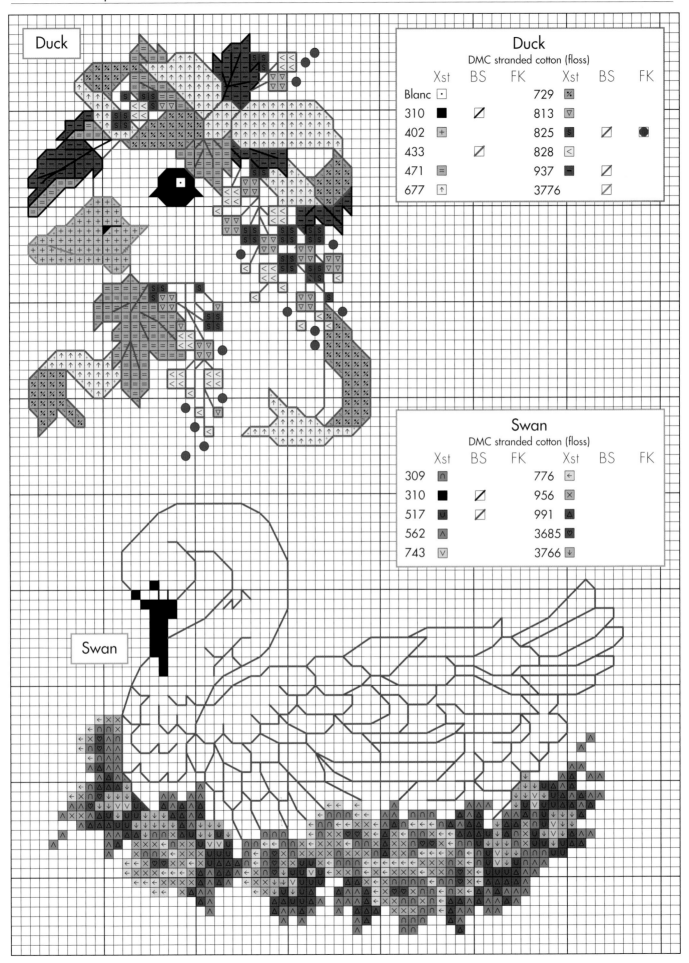

Duck

Duck						
DMC stranded cotton (floss)						
Xst	BS	FK		Xst	BS	FK
Blanc			729			
310			813			
402			825			
433			828			
471			937			
677			3776			

Swan						
DMC stranded cotton (floss)						
Xst	BS	FK		Xst	BS	FK
309			776			
310			956			
517			991			
562			3685			
743			3766			

Swan

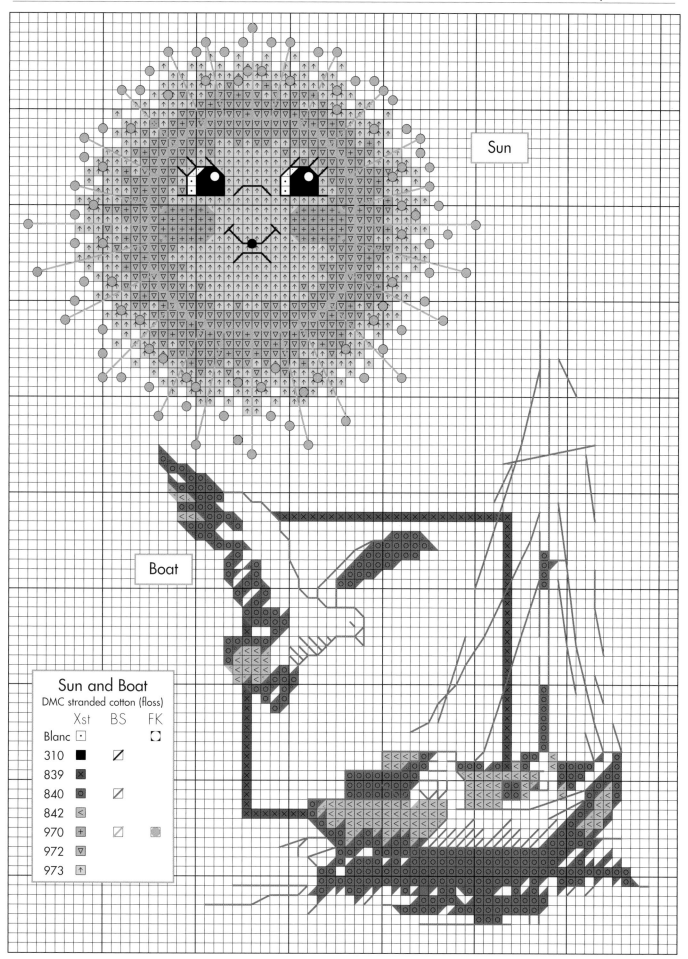

Sun

Boat

Sun and Boat
DMC stranded cotton (floss)

	Xst	BS	FK
Blanc	·		◖
310	■	╱	
839	✕		
840	◉	╱	
842	<		
970	+	╱	▣
972	▽		
973	↑		

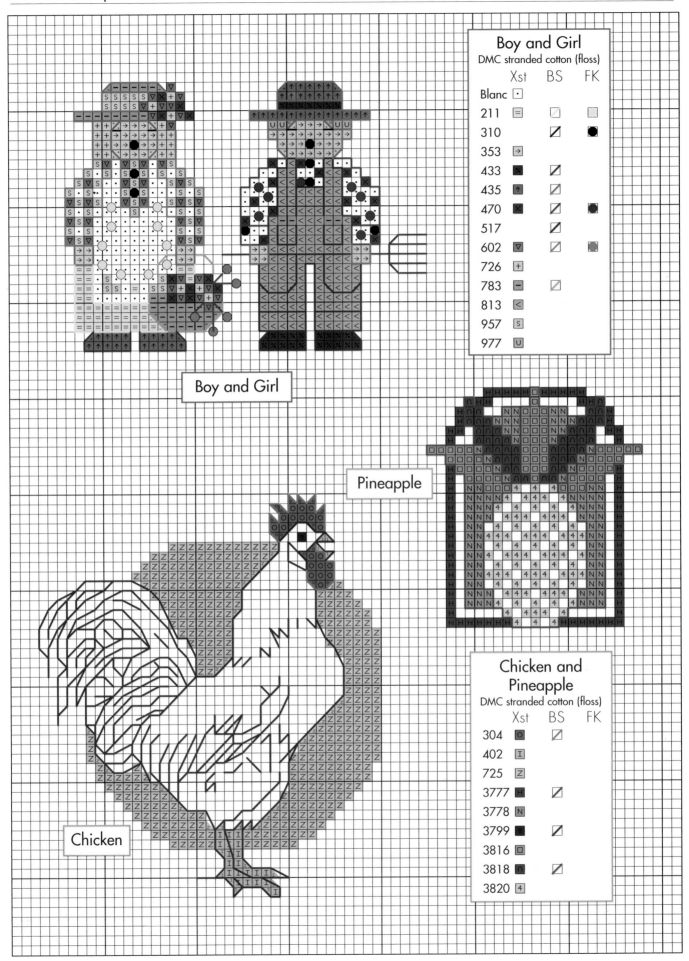

Boy and Girl
DMC stranded cotton (floss)

	Xst	BS	FK
Blanc	·		
211	=	╱	▨
310		╱	●
353	→		
433	▨	╱	
435	↑	╱	
470	✕	╱	■
517		╱	
602	▽	╱	●
726	+		
783	−	╱	
813	<		
957	S		
977	U		

Boy and Girl

Pineapple

Chicken and Pineapple
DMC stranded cotton (floss)

	Xst	BS	FK
304	O	╱	
402	I		
725	Z		
3777	H	╱	
3778	N		
3799	▨	╱	
3816	□		
3818	∩	╱	
3820	4		

Chicken

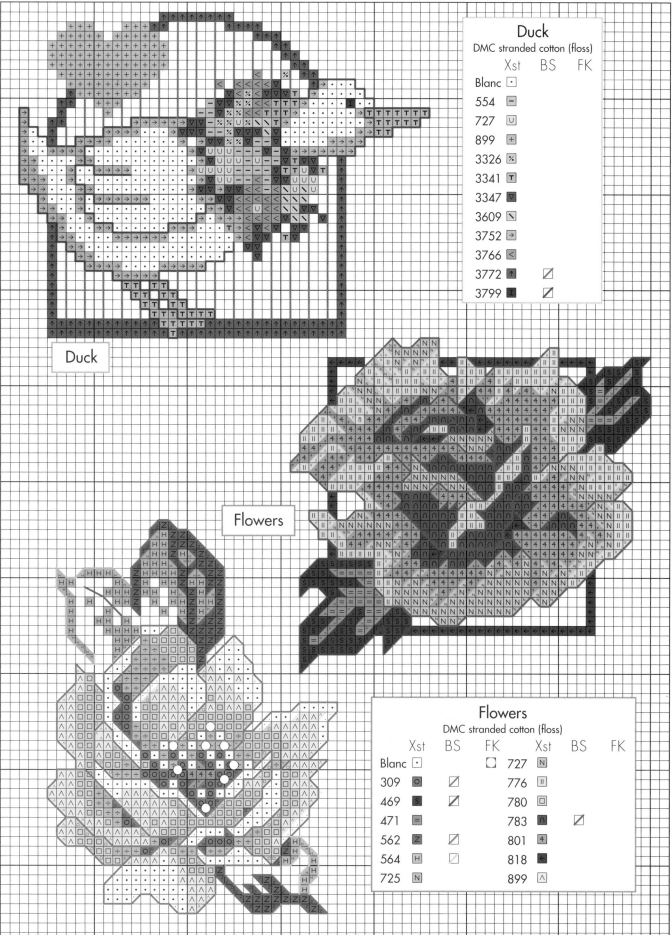

Duck

Flowers

Duck
DMC stranded cotton (floss)

	Xst	BS	FK
Blanc	·		
554	−		
727	U		
899	+		
3326	%		
3341	T		
3347	▽		
3609	◩		
3752	→		
3766	<		
3772	◼	╱	
3799	I	╱	

Flowers
DMC stranded cotton (floss)

	Xst	BS	FK		Xst	BS	FK
Blanc	·		◻	727	N		
309	◉	╱		776	‖		
469	S	╱		780	▣		
471	=			783	◼	╱	
562	Z	╱		801	4		
564	H	╱		818	←		
725	N			899	∧		

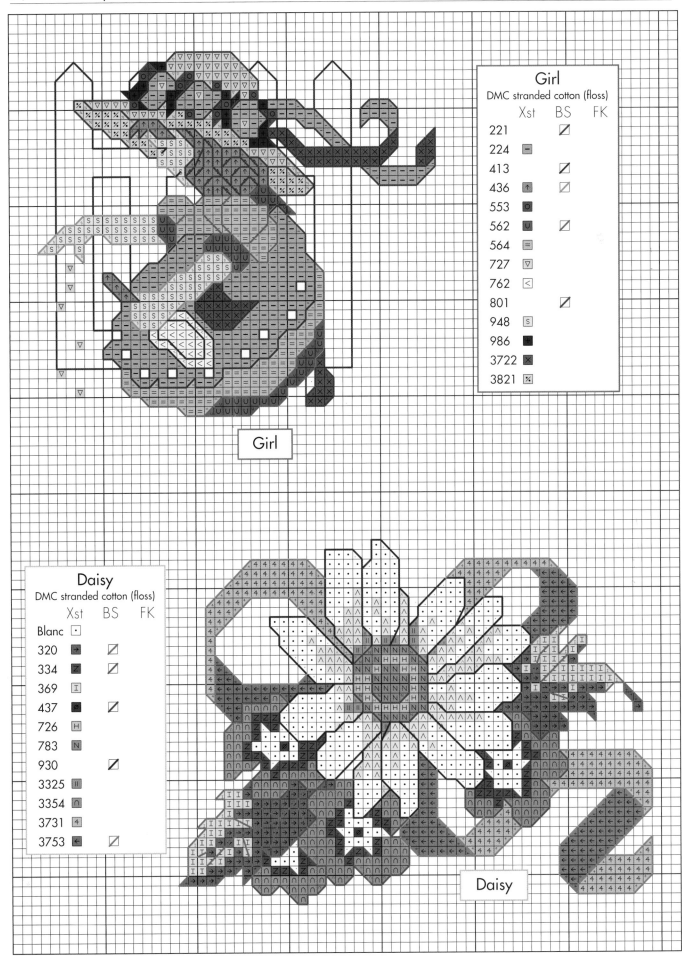

Girl
DMC stranded cotton (floss)

	Xst	BS	FK
221		▨	
224	–		
413		▨	
436	↑	▨	
553	○		
562	U	▨	
564	=		
727	▽		
762	◁		
801		▨	
948	S		
986	■		
3722	✕		
3821	▨		

Girl

Daisy
DMC stranded cotton (floss)

	Xst	BS	FK
Blanc	·		
320	➜	▨	
334	▨	▨	
369	I		
437	◙	▨	
726	H		
783	N		
930		▨	
3325	II		
3354	∩		
3731	◀		
3753	◄	▨	

Daisy

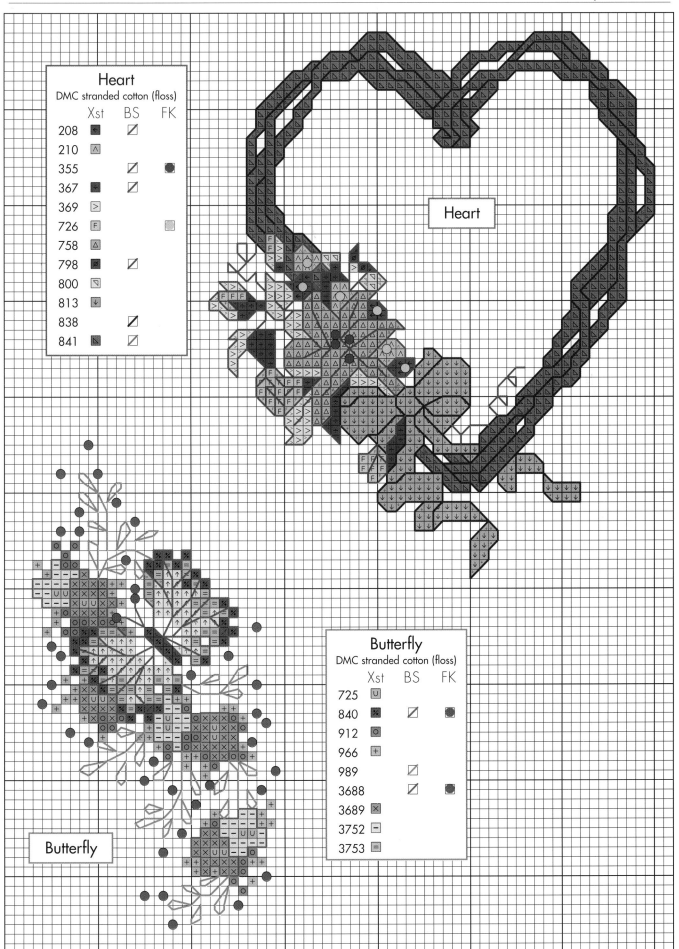

Heart
DMC stranded cotton (floss)

	Xst	BS	FK
208			
210			
355			
367			
369			
726			
758			
798			
800			
813			
838			
841			

Heart

Butterfly
DMC stranded cotton (floss)

	Xst	BS	FK
725			
840			
912			
966			
989			
3688			
3689			
3752			
3753			

Butterfly

Autumn's Riches

Autumn is a time of reflection, a time to think of days gone by and to plan for the winter ahead. The garden is no longer in full growth: leaves are turning brown, and fruit is ripening in the last rays of sunshine. The sampler in this chapter shows the beauty of autumn: the wonderful sounds and shapes that are made by the drying leaves as they rustle and move around in the wind; and the colour in the garden as leaves change from green to orange, and finally brown. On wet days when you are planning next year's garden, the autumnal desk set is a great way to keep your work organised. Then as autumn turns to winter, and you snuggle down in front of a roaring log fire looking at your plans, the fruit cushions and knee warmer will remind you of the beauty that is waiting for you next year

This autumn sampler is stitched on white 14 count Aida fabric using two and three strands of stranded cotton. The chart is on pages 66 and 67.

Autumn Leaves Sampler

This colourful sampler in shades of orange, red and brown is stitched using the chart and key on pages 66 and 67. The poem featured on the sampler, 'Come Little Leaves', captures the spirit of autumn perfectly

- ❧ *Ecru Aida fabric, 14 count 35x42.5cm (14x17in)*
- ❧ *DMC stranded cotton (floss) in the colours listed in the key*
- ❧ *Tapestry needle, No 24*
- ❧ *Picture frame and mount of your choice*

1 Mark the centre of your Aida fabric with tacking stitches and oversew the edges to prevent fraying. Mount the fabric in a frame or embroidery hoop.

2 Work the design from the centre out following the chart and key on pages 66 and 67. The cross stitch is worked in two strands of stranded cotton (floss) and the backstitch in one strand, apart from the poem which is worked in two strands with the words 'author unknown' worked in one strand.

Framing the sampler

1 Wash and press your stitching following the instructions on page 108. Take your work to a framer for mounting and framing, or frame it yourself following the instructions on page 108.

The window panes have been worked in cross stitch using black stranded cotton (floss), and then the diamond leading is added in two strands of white.

Autumn Fruits Cushions

Apples, pears, grapes and berries have been used to decorate these attractive wool blanketing cushions, which are finished with large wooden buttons and blanket stitch

- ❧ Cream Zweigart Belfast linen, 28 count two pieces 12x12cm (4³/₄x4³/₄in)
- ❧ DMC stranded cotton (floss) in the colours listed in the key
- ❧ Blue wool blanketing, one piece 30x35.5cm (12x14in), and one 30x32.5cm (12x13in)
- ❧ Cushion pad
- ❧ Wooden buttons 2cm (³/₄in)
- ❧ Cream crochet cotton and large eyed needle
- ❧ Tapestry needle, No 24
- ❧ Blue sewing thread and needle
- ❧ White tacking thread

1 Mark the centre of each square of Belfast linen with tacking stitches and oversew around the fabric edges to prevent fraying. Mount each piece in an embroidery hoop.

2 Work a large pear or large apple in the middle of each piece of Belfast linen, following the charts and key on pages 68 and 69. Use two strands of stranded cotton (floss) for the cross stitch, and one strand for the backstitch and french knots, working each stitch over two threads of fabric.

Making up the cushion

1 The cushion is made from two pieces of blue wool blanketing. The pleat on the front of the cushion finished with buttons is just for decoration. You can either add a zip to the side seam for inserting the cushion pad, or insert it through a gap left in the seam which is then sewn up with small neat stitches. On the larger of the two pieces of blanketing make a 1.25cm

(¹/₂in) pleat across the fabric, parallel with a shorter side and slightly closer to one edge. Pin then tack the pleat in place. The fabric will now be the same size as the other piece of blanketing.

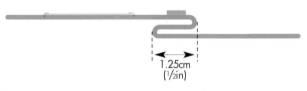

1.25cm
(¹/₂in)

The pleat is made across one piece of blanketing, so that the front of the cushion is divided into two unequal parts.

2 Turn under the edges of one piece of stitched linen 1cm (³/₈in), press then tack in place. Tack the stitched linen square on to one piece of blanketing, on the larger side of the pleat.

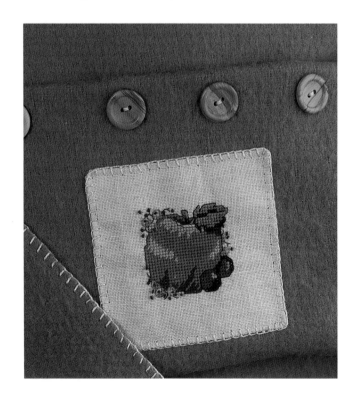

3 Using crochet cotton, blanket stitch around the edge of the stitched linen square to hold it firmly on to the cushion.

4 Place the two pieces of blanketing right sides together, tack and then stitch around the outer edges with a 1cm (³⁄₈in) seam allowance, but leaving a small gap on one side for turning. Turn the cushion

cover to the right side, through the gap left in the stitching. To make the cushion pad easier to remove, a zip can be stitched in the gap. Insert the cushion pad and sew up the gap.

5 Sew four equally spaced buttons along the pleat on the front of the cushion. Remove the tacking stitches holding down the pleat.

Autumn Fruits Knee Blanket

Leave this useful knee blanket over the arm of your favourite chair, so that it will be handy on chilly evenings. Decorated with fruit and berries, it will cheer you up even on the coldest autumn day

- ❧ *Cream Zweigart Belfast linen, 28 count 65.5x10.5cm (25³⁄₄x4¹⁄₈in)*
- ❧ *DMC stranded cotton (floss) in the colours listed in the key*
- ❧ *Blue wool blanketing, 112x66cm (45x26in)*
- ❧ *Cream crochet cotton and large eyed needle*
- ❧ *Tapestry needle, No 24*
- ❧ *White tacking thread*

1 Oversew the edges of the Belfast linen to prevent it fraying, and then blanket stitch the edges of the wool blanketing using crochet cotton. Sew a row of tacking stitches parallel with the long edge, and

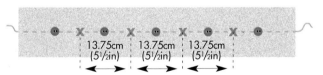

Make a row of tacking stitches across the middle of the linen, then make nine single tacking stitches to show the centre of each stitched motif and button.

across the middle of the linen fabric. Make nine tacking stitches along this line for the four fruit motifs and five buttons. Each stitch will be the centre point of

a fruit or button: the fruit motifs should be 13.75cm (5¹⁄₂in) between centre points, with the buttons mid-way between.

2 Work the four fruit motifs across the width of the Belfast linen, so that the centre of each design matches up with a tacking stitch, and following the charts and keys on pages 68 and 69. Use two strands of stranded cotton (floss) for the cross stitch, and one strand for the backstitch and french knots, working each stitch over two threads of fabric.

3 Turn over the top and bottom edges of the linen by 1cm (³⁄₈in), and the sides edges to fit the width of the blanket. Tack the stitched linen panel on to the blanket, a little way down from the top edge. Using crochet cotton, stitch around the edge of the panel with large running stitches to hold it firmly to the blanket. Sew buttons between the motifs at the points marked with tacking stitches.

Wooden buttons and a mock pleat have been used to decorate these modern looking cushions and blanket.

Autumnal Note Block

This useful note block is a great way of making sure you can always find paper and a pencil on your desk. The design is decorated with an initial taken from the alphabet on page 106

❧ *White Aida fabric, 14 count 11x33cm (4½ x13in)*
❧ *Iron-on vilene 11x33cm (4½ x13in)*
❧ *DMC stranded cotton (floss) in the colours listed in the key*
❧ *Clear plastic note block*
❧ *Tapestry needle, No 24*

1 The design for the note block should be stitched three times to cover each side of the note block. To do this, remove the plastic divider from the note block and lay it down on to the Aida fabric. Make a small mark on the top and bottom edge of the Aida in line with the corner folds in the plastic – when assembled these are the two corners at the back of the

note block. Your Aida fabric is divided into three sections: the middle section where the centre is marked with tacking stitches; and the left and right sections, where the design will need to start three squares away from the corner folds. When you have found the starting points, measure back to find the

The fabric is divided into three, with pencil marks to show the corner folds of the plastic divider. Start stitching each block three squares away from the pencil line.

centre point of each section, then mark these points with tacking stitches. The fabric should be cut to size after the design has been stitched. Oversew the edges of the Aida, and mount it in an embroidery hoop.

2 Work the design three times, starting at the centre points marked on the fabric with tacking stitches. The cross stitch is worked in two strands of stranded cotton (floss) and the backstitch in two strands for the vine stems, and one for the rest of the design.

3 Apply iron-on vilene to the back of the design. Lay the stitching design side up on the table. Position the plastic divider over the stitching, so that the folds correspond with the pencil marks at the top and bottom of the Aida. Draw around the divider lightly with pencil, then cut around this line. Slide the design and the divider back into the note block.

Autumnal Gift Cards and Tags

These pretty gift cards are simple to make using card blanks and handmade paper. The ivy leaf shaped gift tags can be made using the template on page 106

- White Aida fabric, 14 count 25x7.3cm (9¾ x3in)
- DMC stranded cotton (floss) in the colours listed in the key
- Iron-on vilene
- Greetings card blanks, larger than the designs
- Hand-made paper and fabric glue
- Metallic card and parcel cord
- Tapestry needle, No 24

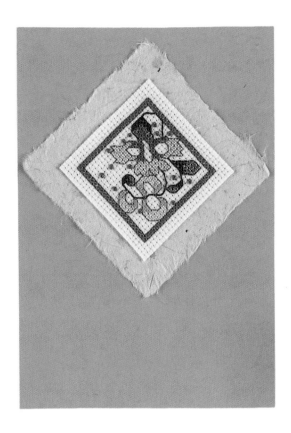

1 Oversew the edges of the Aida fabric to prevent fraying, and mount it in an embroidery hoop.

2 Work the designs on to the fabric following the charts and key on pages 70 and 71. The cross stitch is worked in two strands of stranded cotton (floss), the backstitch for the vine stems in two strands and the rest of the backstitch in one strand.

Making the cards

1 Cut out the three card motifs, leaving three squares of blank Aida around each design. Apply iron-on vilene to the back of each design. Tear a square of hand-made paper slightly Larger than each design. Glue the paper and the design on to the front of a card blank.

This ivy leaf shaped tag has been made using the template on page 107.

Making the tags

1 Apply vilene to the back of the tag designs in the same way as for the cards. Cut around each tag design leaving a few squares of blank fabric.

2 Using the template on page 107, cut an ivy leaf shape from metallic card. Glue the stitching on to the tag. Punch a hole at the top of the tag and thread with gold parcel cord.

Autumnal Folder and Ruler

The design for the folder and ruler is finished with letters taken from the alphabet on page 106. Use graph paper to plot the ruler design before you begin stitching

- ❦ White Aida fabric, 14 count – ruler 3x35cm (2x14in), folder 12x20cm (5x8in)
- ❦ DMC stranded cotton (floss) in the colours listed in the key
- ❦ Iron-on vilene
- ❦ Clear plastic ruler
- ❦ Folder
- ❦ Brown ribbon and fabric glue
- ❦ Tapestry needle, No 24
- ❦ Graph paper and pencil

Stitching the ruler

1 Using the template provided with the ruler, work out the exact size of the Aida fabric needed for the design, and mark it on to a sheet of graph paper. Plot the border and corner designs on to the graph paper using the chart and key on page 70 and 71. Using the alphabet on page 106, plot your chosen name on to the graph paper, making sure the letters are evenly spaced, and central between the border edges and the corner designs.

2 Mark the centre of the Aida, then oversew around the edges to prevent fraying. Work from the centre out, following your graph paper chart, and using two strands of stranded cotton (floss) for the cross stitch, two for the backstitch vine stems, and one for the remainder of the design.

3 Apply iron-on vilene to the back of the stitching, then cut around the design just outside the border edge. Position the design in the ruler, and then snap on the clear front panel.

Stitching the folder

1 Mark the centre of your Aida fabric with tacking stitches and oversew the edges to prevent fraying. Mount the fabric in a frame or embroidery hoop.

2 Work the design from the centre out following the chart and key on pages 70 and 71. The initial is added to the design using the alphabet chart on page 106. The cross stitch is worked in two strands of stranded cotton (floss) and the backstitch in two strands for the vine stems, and one for the rest of the design.

3 Wash and press your stitching following the instructions on page 108. Apply iron-on vilene to the back of the stitching. Cut away the Aida either side of the design, one square outside the border edge, but leaving the Aida at the top and bottom.

4 Glue the stitched panel on to the front of the folder, wrapping the excess fabric at the top and bottom edges over on to the inside flap. Glue fine brown ribbon on to the front of the folder either side of the design. Glue a piece of ribbon on to the inside front and back cover flaps.

5 Cut two pieces of hand-made paper the same size as the inside front and back folder flaps. Glue the paper inside the folder covering the ribbon ends. Tie the ribbon ends into a bow.

The letters on the folder, note block and ruler are stitched using the alphabet on page 106.

Autumn Sampler

DMC stranded cotton (floss)

■	310	Backstitch	
S	317	◪	Blanc
T	318	◪	310
↑	355	◪	356
U	356	◪	838
→	402	◪	3777
4	433	French knots	
◪	434	●	3777
←	435		
∩	437		
F	469		
I	721		
N	738		
<	743		
⟍	762		
Z	783		
■	838		
%	839		
O	840		
▽	841		
∧	931		
∅	936		
H	973		
≠	3347		
>	3348		
÷	3752		
X	3777		
=	3778		

Blanket – Blackberries

Blanket – Thistle

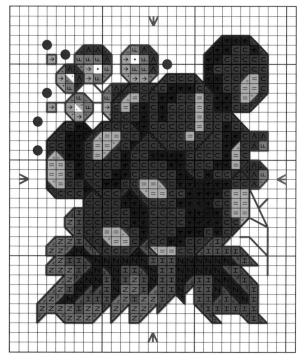

Blanket – Grapes

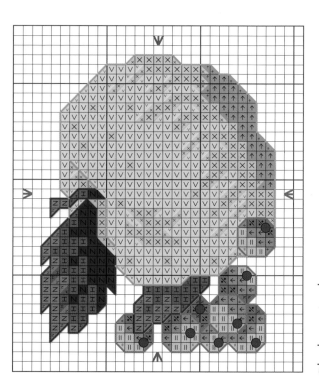

Blanket – Apple

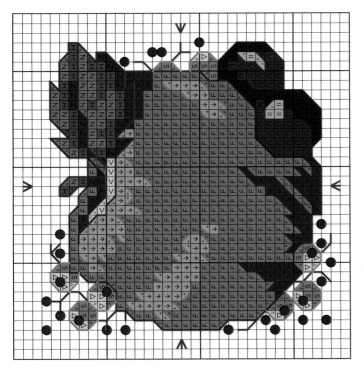

Cushion – Apple

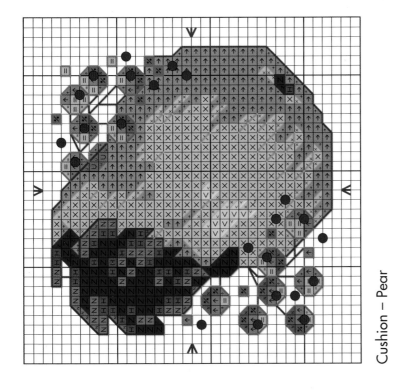

Cushion – Pear

Blanket and Cushions

DMC stranded cotton (floss)

·	Blanc	▲	554	◣	839	⊟	3374
▲	221	✖	720	✚	841		Backstitch
⊩	223	←	721	◪	918	◢	407
→	224	✕	725	⊤	921	◩	550
↓	225	∨	727	◼	986	◩	720
⊫	402	↑	729	⊞	988	◩	729
⊔	407	◼	797	◪	989	◩	797
◼	550	S	799	⊔	3341	◩	799
◧	552	▷	800	⊙	3373	◩	839

◪	918		French knots
◪	986	●	797
◪	3773	●	839
		●	918

Cards

Gift Tags

Note Block

Ruler

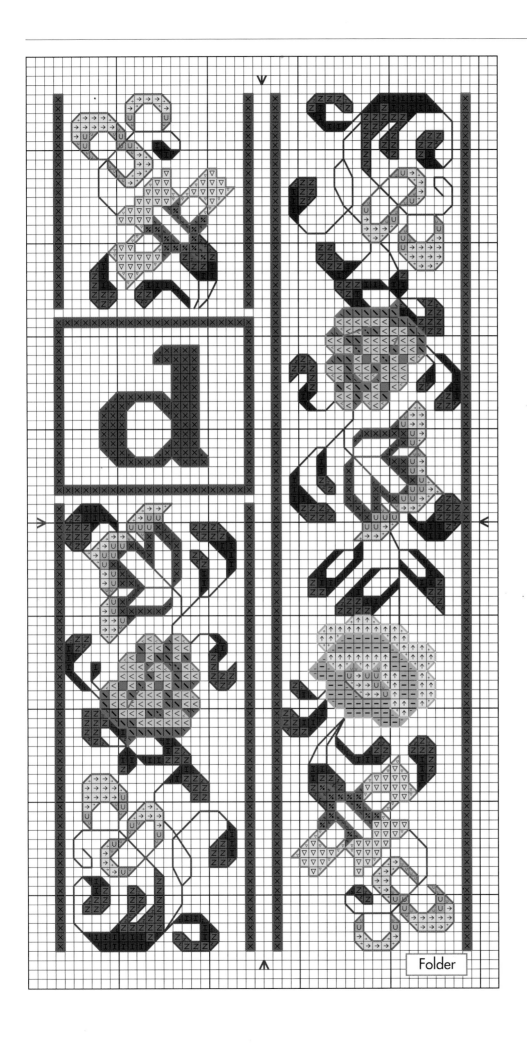

Autumn Desk Set

DMC stranded cotton (floss)

◣	208
◁	210
✕	434
⋃	437
→	739
⊠	826
▽	827
■	3345
⊠	3347
–	3688
↑	3689

Backstitch

◿	208
◿	434
◿	826
◿	3345
◿	3688

French knots

⬤	434

Folder

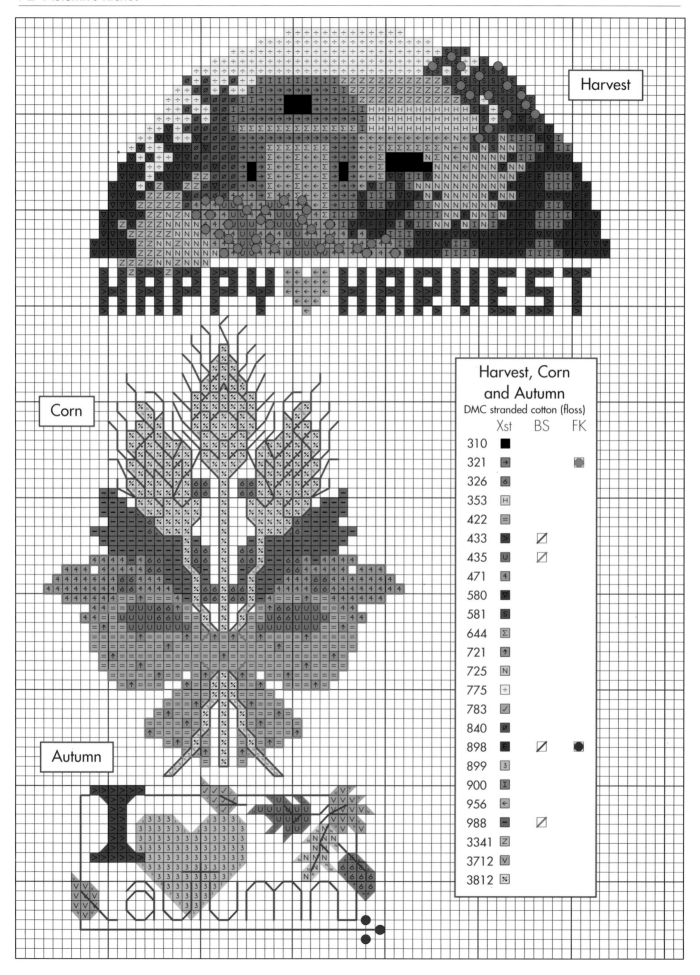

Harvest

Corn

Autumn

Harvest, Corn and Autumn
DMC stranded cotton (floss)

	Xst	BS	FK
310	■		
321	→		●
326	6		
353	H		
422	=		
433	>	◿	
435	U	◿	
471	4		
580	▽		
581	S		
644	Σ		
721	↑		
725	N		
775	÷		
783	✓		
840	∅		
898	F	◿	●
899	3		
900	I		
956	←		
988	—	◿	
3341	Z		
3712	V		
3812	%		

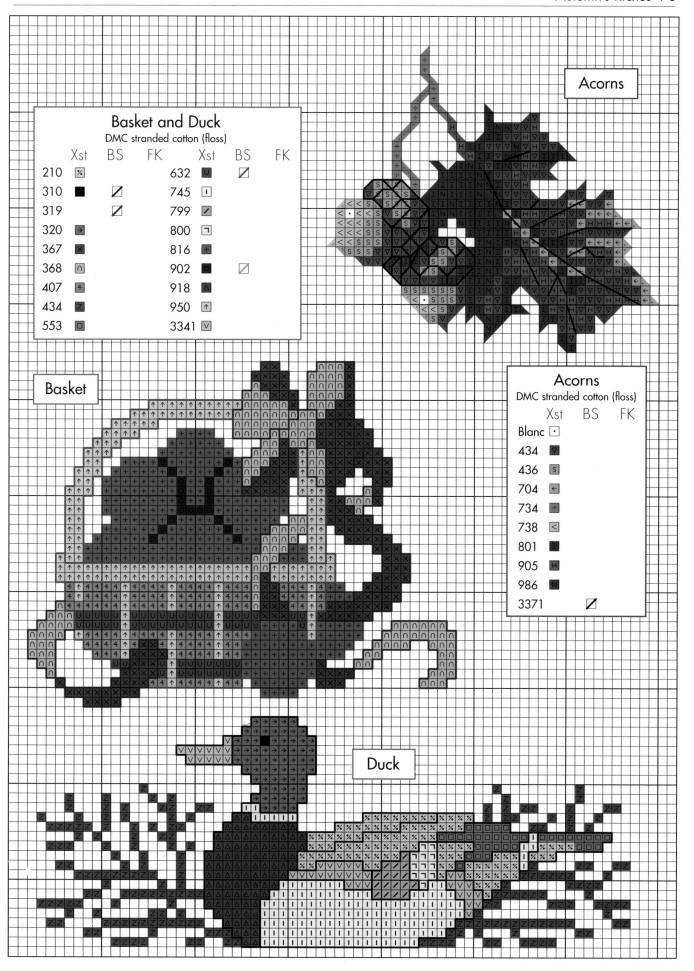

Acorns

Basket and Duck
DMC stranded cotton (floss)

	Xst	BS	FK		Xst	BS	FK
210	▨			632	⊔		╱
310	■	╱		745	I		
319		╱		799	◪		
320	▸			800	⌐		
367	✕			816	＋		
368	∩			902	◼		╱
407	↊			918	▲		
434	☒			950	↑		
553	▢			3341	▽		

Basket

Acorns
DMC stranded cotton (floss)

	Xst	BS	FK
Blanc	·		
434	▽		
436	S		
704	←		
734	＋		
738	<		
801	I		
905	H		
986	N		
3371		╱	

Duck

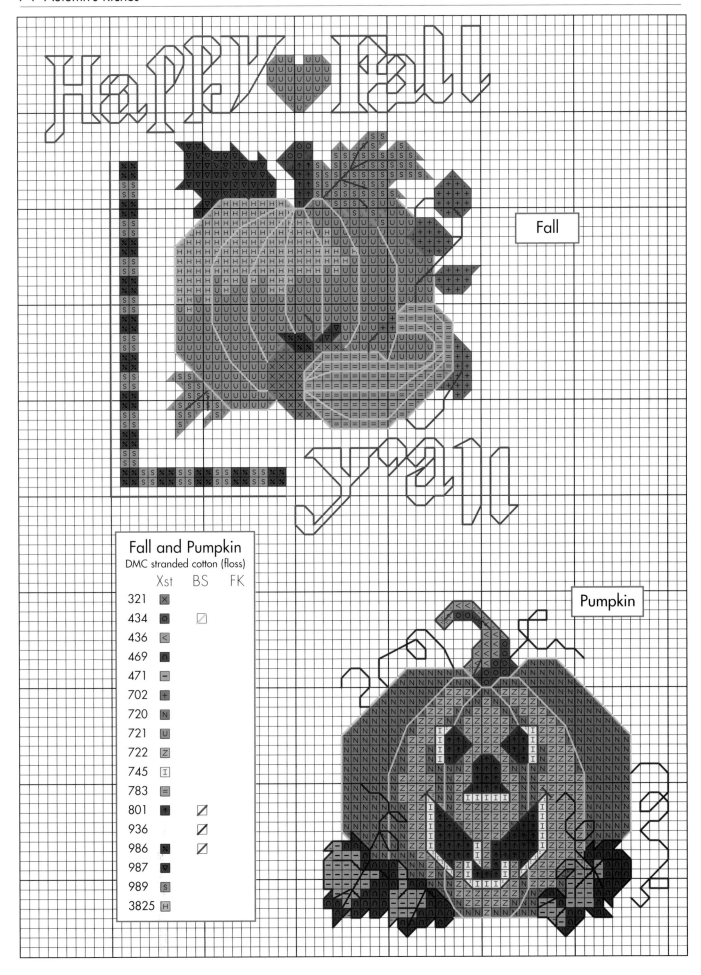

Fall

Pumpkin

Fall and Pumpkin
DMC stranded cotton (floss)

	Xst	BS	FK
321	☒		
434	◙	▧	
436	◀		
469	◪		
471	▬		
702	⊞		
720	N		
721	U		
722	Z		
745	I		
783	▤		
801	◼	▧	
936		▧	
986	▨	▧	
987	▽		
989	S		
3825	H		

Scarecrows
DMC stranded cotton (floss)

	Xst	BS	FK		Xst	BS	FK
Blanc	·			809	−		
310	■	╱		894	S		
321	▽	╱		900	←	╱	
434	U	╱		905	■	╱	
436	+	╱		907	▨		
725	=			3341	⊠		
798	◎						

Scarecrows

Pumpkin

Pumpkin
DMC stranded cotton (floss)

	Xst	BS	FK		Xst	BS	FK
402	I			3362	▣	╱	
435	Z	╱		3363	▥		
437	H			3364	∩		
739	Σ			3778	F		
801	N	╱					

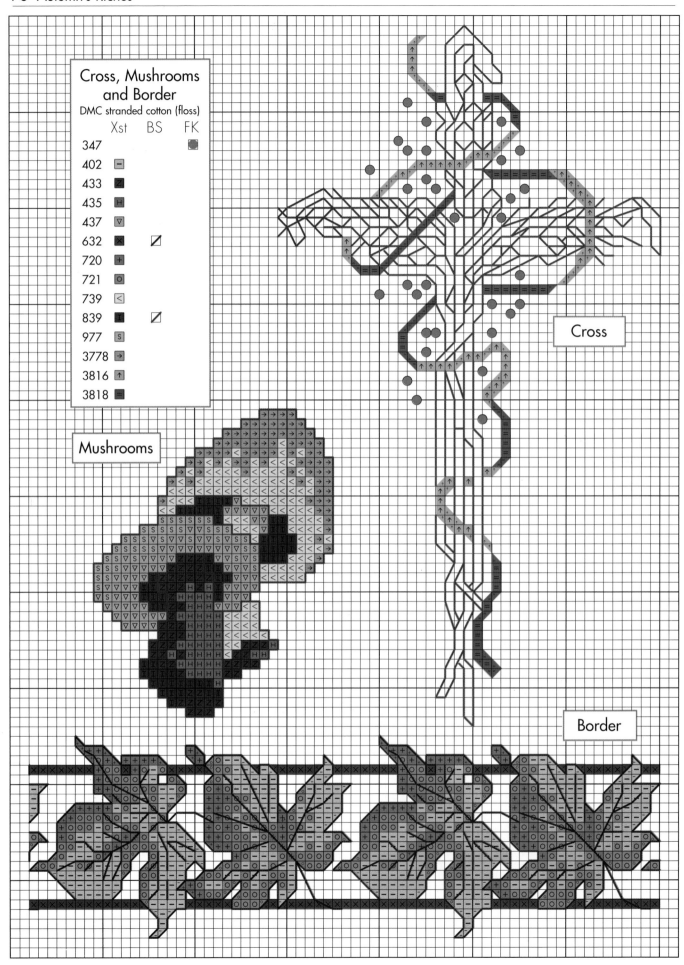

Cross, Mushrooms and Border
DMC stranded cotton (floss)

	Xst	BS	FK
347			●
402	–		
433	◪		
435	H		
437	▽		
632	✕	⧄	
720	+		
721	○		
739	<		
839	■	⧄	
977	S		
3778	→		
3816	↑		
3818	=		

Cross

Mushrooms

Border

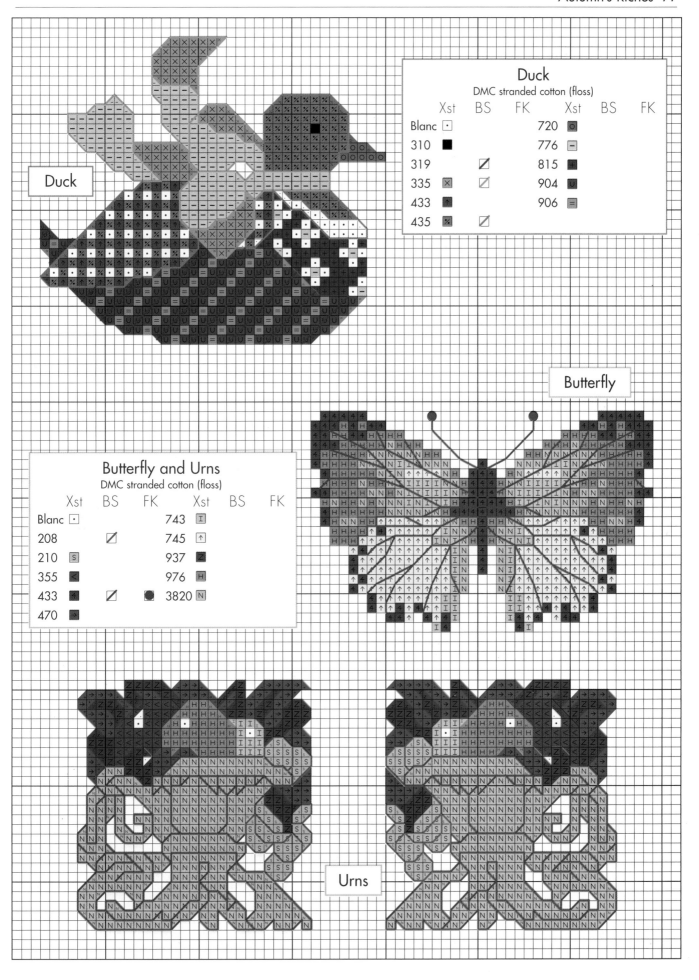

Duck

Duck
DMC stranded cotton (floss)

	Xst	BS	FK		Xst	BS	FK
Blanc	·			720	⊙		
310	■			776	–		
319		⊘		815	⊞		
335	⊠	⊘		904	U		
433	↑			906	=		
435	⊘	⊘					

Butterfly

Butterfly and Urns
DMC stranded cotton (floss)

	Xst	BS	FK		Xst	BS	FK
Blanc	·			743	I		
208		⊘		745	↑		
210	S			937	◪		
355	◤			976	H		
433	◼	⊘	●	3820	N		
470	→						

Urns

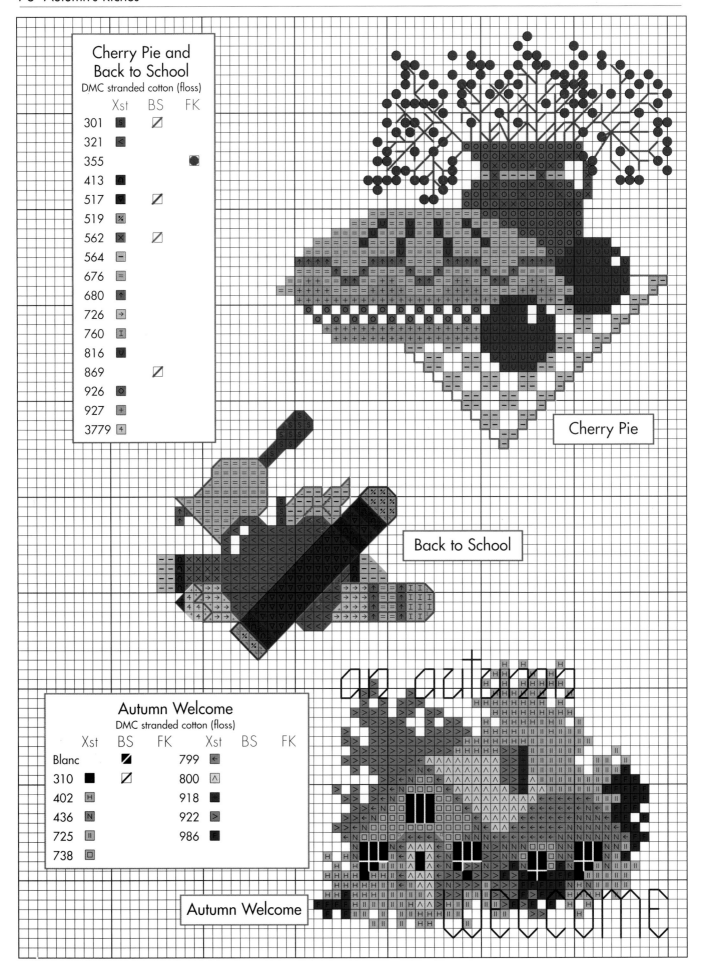

Cherry Pie and Back to School
DMC stranded cotton (floss)

	Xst	BS	FK
301			
321			
355			
413			
517			
519			
562			
564			
676			
680			
726			
760			
816			
869			
926			
927			
3779			

Cherry Pie

Back to School

Autumn Welcome
DMC stranded cotton (floss)

	Xst	BS	FK		Xst	BS	FK
Blanc				799			
310				800			
402				918			
436				922			
725				986			
738							

Autumn Welcome

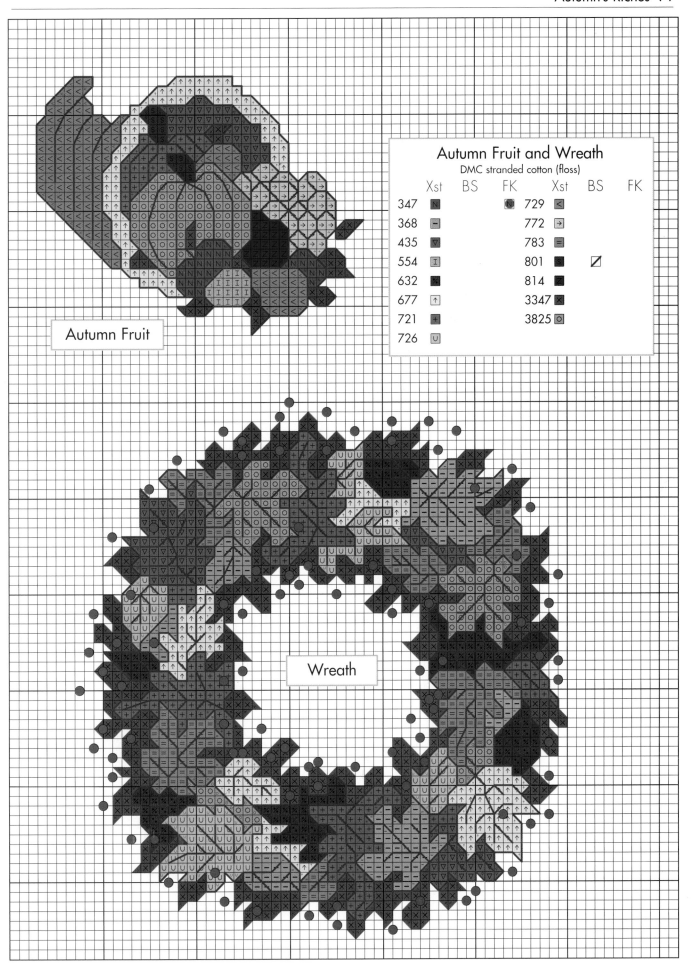

Autumn Fruit and Wreath
DMC stranded cotton (floss)

	Xst	BS	FK		Xst	BS	FK
347	N		N	729	<		
368	−			772	→		
435	▽			783	=		
554	I			801	■	⊘	
632	▨			814	▨		
677	↑			3347	✕		
721	+			3825	⊙		
726	U						

Autumn Fruit

Wreath

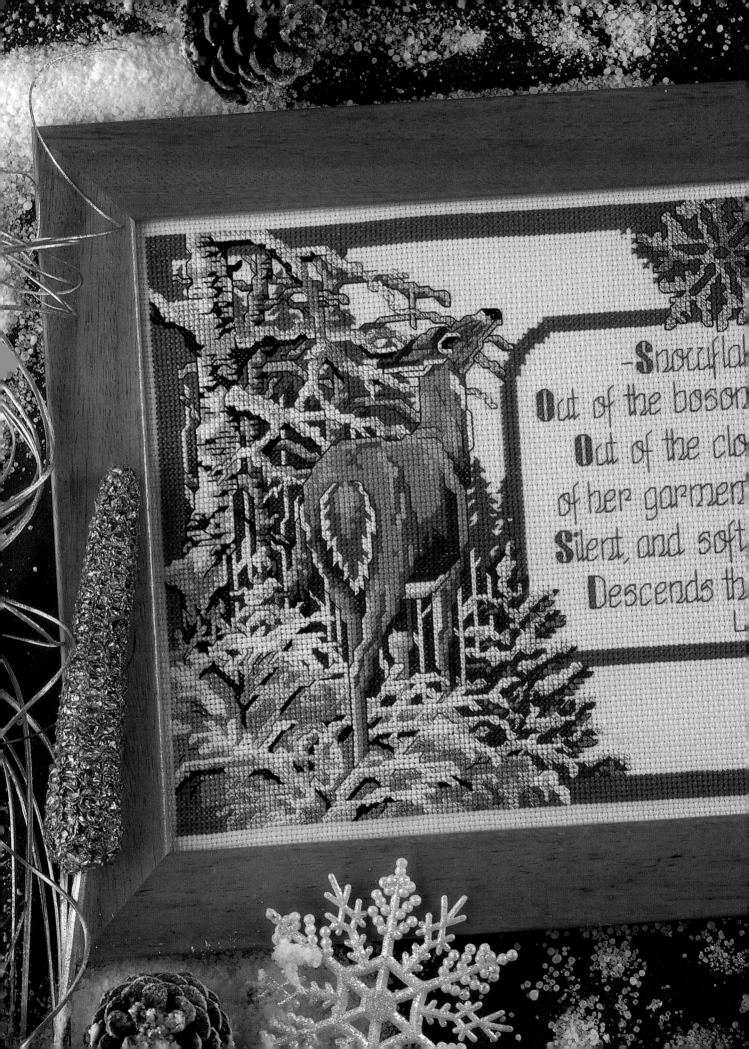

Winter's Wonders

Winter is a time of planning and great merriment. While you stitch and bake for Christmas, you think about projects you would like to do in the warmer months of Spring. Outside the countryside is tucked up warm under its snowy white blanket. Trees are laden with snow, and the frost on the hedgerows glistens in the weak winter sunshine. The sampler in this chapter shows a fawn pausing in a woodland clearing. The colour of his coat stands out well against the winter snow, as he rests before moving on through the trees.

This year why not make a special Christmas keepsake: the stocking with Santa's jolly face or a pretty hanging tree decoration. Both are sure to become family favourites, making them the centre point of your Christmas festivities for many years to come

The snow on this woodland sampler is stitched using Kreinek blending filament to make it sparkle. The chart can be found on pages 90 and 91.

Winter Woodland Sampler

Kreinek blending filament has been used with the stranded cotton (floss) on some areas of this sampler to make it sparkle. The large snowflakes on the right would make a pretty hanging decoration or greetings cards

- ❧ *White Aida fabric, 14 count 35x42.5cm (14x17in)*
- ❧ *DMC stranded cotton (floss) in the colours listed in the key*
- ❧ *Kreinek blending filament colour 014 and 100HL*
- ❧ *Tapestry needle, No 24*
- ❧ *Picture frame and mount of your choice*

1 Mark the centre of your Aida fabric with tacking stitches and oversew the edges to prevent fraying. Mount the fabric in a frame.

2 Work the design from the centre out following the chart and key on pages 90 and 91. The cross stitch is worked in two strands of stranded cotton (floss) and the backstitch in one strand. Two strands of

Kreinek blending filament colour 100L are used with the white stranded cotton (floss) on snowy areas in the foreground, but not on the tree trunks or the fawn. One strand of Kreinek colour 014 is mixed with DMC stranded cotton (floss) colours 813 and 828 for the snow and the snowflakes.

Framing the sampler

1 Wash and press your stitching following the instructions on page 108. Take your work to a framer for mounting and framing, or frame it yourself following the instructions on page 108.

The snow is worked in stranded cotton (floss) mixed with blending filament. The white tree trunks and the markings on the fawn are stitched using just stranded cotton (floss).

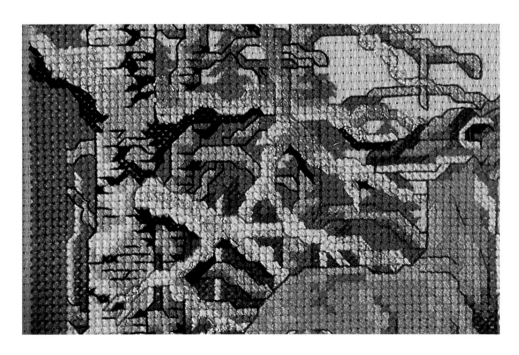

Christmas Tree Decorations

These pretty hanging tree decorations are stitched on cream Belfast linen. All the decorations have been trimmed with gold cord, pearls and red fabric roses

- Cream Zweigart Belfast linen, 32 count – one piece 10x10cm (4x4in) for the Santa; six pieces each 10x10cm (4x4in) for the musical instrument; three pieces each 10x12.5 (4x5in) for the pear tree
- DMC stranded cotton (floss) in the colours listed in the key
- Toy stuffing, thick cardboard, green felt
- Selection of beads, pearls, fine red ribbon and ribbon roses
- Gold parcel cord 1.6m (1³/₄yds)
- Iron-on vilene
- Fabric glue
- Tapestry needle No 24,
- Large eyed needle
- Metallic sewing thread
- White sewing thread and needle
- White tacking thread

Stitching the Santa decoration

1 Mark the centre of the linen with tacking stitches and oversew around the fabric edges to prevent fraying. Mount the linen in an embroidery hoop.

2 Work the Santa design from the centre out following the chart and key on pages 92 and 93. Use two strands of stranded cotton (floss) for the cross stitch and two strands for the backstitch, working each stitch over two threads of fabric.

3 Apply iron-on vilene to the back of the stitching, then mark a 7.5cm (3in) circle on the fabric keeping the design in the centre of the circle.

4 Using the template on page 107, cut the shape from thick cardboard. Cut a small piece of green felt just larger than the heart shaped area at the bottom of the cardboard hanger. Glue the felt on to the hanger, wrapping the excess felt on to the back. Using the same template as for the cardboard hanger, cut a shape from green felt. Glue the felt on to the back of the cardboard.

5 Carefully position the circular Santa design on to the front of the hanger, and glue it in place. Glue beads and ribbon roses on to the heart shaped felt area at the bottom of the hanger. Glue two rows of gold cord on to the edge of the decoration, twisting the outer ring at the top to form a hanger.

Stitching the musical decoration

1 The musical decoration is a cube made up of six squares of linen. The musical design can be stitched on one, or all six sides of the linen cube; or several different designs could be used. Oversew the edges of the linen squares, and then mount them in an embroidery hoop.

2 Work the musical instrument from the centre out following the chart and key on pages 92 and 93. Use two strands of stranded cotton (floss) for the cross stitch, two strands for the backstitch and one for the french knots, working each stitch over two threads of fabric.

3 When all the squares have been stitched, apply iron-on vilene to the back of the linen. Cut each square of linen down to 8cm (3¼in), keeping the design exactly in the centre of the fabric. Join four stitched squares together along one edge with a 1cm (⅜in) seam allowance. Join the edges at the beginning and end together to form a complete circle of fabric. Press the seams so that the fabric is shaped like a cube without a top or bottom.

4 On the two remaining squares of stitched linen fabric, turn over the edges by 1cm (⅜in) and press in place. Working on the wrong side of the fabric, pin then sew the linen squares on to the top and bottom of the cube, leaving one seam unstitched for turning to the right side. Turn the cube through to the right side. Stuff the cube with toy stuffing, until it is firm but not overfull.

5 Lay gold cord along the seam lines of the cube, tucking the starting end into the corner of the open side. Work on one small area at a time, securing the cord on to the cube with a couching stitch (see page 108) and using metallic thread, but leaving the last seam to be couched the open side. Sew up the open seam, leaving just a small gap at the corner where the cord end was inserted. Couch the cord on to the final seam. Push the cord end into the gap before sewing it up.

6 The tassel at the bottom of the cube is made by cutting a bundle of 10cm (4in) lengths of metallic thread. Lay a piece of slightly thicker cord horizontally on the table. On top of this lay the bundle of metallic thread vertically, so that the middle of the bundle is intersected by the length of thicker thread. Take both ends of this thread, and tie a knot so that the bundle of thread is held firmly together.

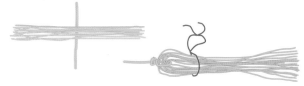

Tie a bundle of gold thread together with a thicker gold thread. Bring the bundle ends together, then tie a length of thread around the bundle, just down from the folded end.

Bring the thread ends in the bundle together. Wrap a length of gold thread around the bundle several times, just down from the folded end of the bundle. Finish

This pretty selection of Christmas cards and decorations could all be made into either hangers or cards.

with a knot. Attach the tassel to the bottom corner of the cube with a few small stitches.

7 To make a hanger, thread a large eyed needle with a length of fine ribbon. Make a stitch into the top corner of the cube, then tie the ribbon ends together to secure the ribbon to the cube.

8 Decorate the corners of the cube with pearls, beads, ribbon loops and ribbon roses.

Stitching the pear tree decoration

1 The pear tree decoration is made from three ovals of Belfast linen. To complete the decoration the design will need to be stitched three times. The oval shapes should be cut from the fabric after the designs has been stitched. Oversew the edges of the linen and mark the centre point on each rectangle with tacking stitches, before mounting them in an embroidery hoop.

2 Work the pear tree design from the centre out following the chart and key on pages 92 and 93. Use two strands of stranded cotton (floss) for the cross stitch, two strands for the backstitch and one for the french knots, working each stitch over two threads of fabric.

3 When the design has been stitched three times, apply iron-on vilene to the back of the linen fabric. Using the trace on page 107 as a guide, cut three identical oval shapes from the stitched fabric pieces. Mark the centre top and bottom points on to each oval of fabric with a tacking stitch.

4 Lay two stitched linen ovals right sides together. With a 1cm (⅜in) seam allowance, join the ovals together down one side from the centre top to bottom. Lay the partly constructed decoration flat on your ironing board, fold the unstitched half of the top fabric oval over on to the stitched half, press in place.

5 Lay the remaining stitched oval on top of the other two. Join the third oval to the edges of the other two, with a 1cm (⅜in) seam allowance, leaving a gap on one side for turning and a small gap at the top and bottom of the decoration. Trim away the excess fabric from around the edges of the ovals, then turn the decoration through to the right side. Sew up the gap left in the side seam.

6 Lay gold cord along the seam lines around each oval shape, tucking the cord ends into the opening left at the top or bottom of the decoration. Work on one small area at a time, securing the cord with a couching stitch (see page 108) and using metallic thread.

7 Add a ribbon hanger to the top of the decoration, then sew up the small gaps left at the top and bottom. To finish the decoration, add a ribbon hanger to the top and a tassel to the bottom, following the tassel making instructions on page 84.

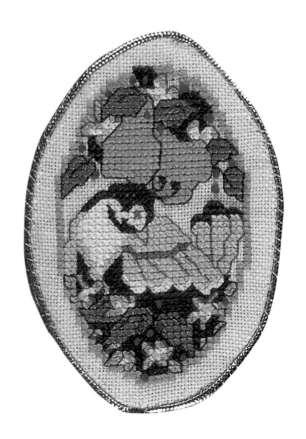

Christmas Cards and Tags

There can be no nicer gift at Christmas than a handstitched greeting, and these pretty cards and tags are a wonderful way to say 'Happy Christmas' to special friends

❧ *Cream Zweigart Belfast linen , 32 count – two pieces 9x11cm (4x4½in) for the cards; two pieces 5x5cm (2x2in) for the tags; one piece 5cm (2in) X flowerpot diameter*

❧ *DMC stranded cotton (floss) in the colours listed in the key*

❧ *Card with a 6.25x8cm (2½x3¼in) rectangular aperture for each design*

❧ *Gift tags 5x5cm (2x2in)*

❧ *Iron-on vilene, green crochet cotton*

❧ *Tapestry needle No 24*

❧ *Fabric glue, double-sided tape*

❧ *2.5cm (1in) wide length of thin card*

❧ *Terracotta plant pot*

Making up the cards

1 Work each card design in the same way as for the decorations, following the charts and key on pages 92 and 93. Use two strands of stranded cotton (floss) for the cross stitch, two strands for the backstitch and one for the french knots, working each stitch over two threads of fabric. On the tree design, the backstitch stars and the star at the top of the tree should be worked in two strands. Mount the design in a rectangular card, following the card making up instructions on page 108.

Making up the tags

1 Work the tag designs in the same way as the cards, following the chart and key on pages 92 and 93. Apply iron-on vilene to the back of the stitching, then cut a 4cm (1½in) diameter circle from the fabric keeping the design in the centre. Glue the design on to the front of a gift tag. Lay crochet cotton around the edge of the design, and glue in place.

Making up the plant pot band

1 Cut a length of linen 5cm (2in) wide and the circumference of your plant pot. Stitch the design in the same way as for the cards and tags, repeating it several times to cover the linen strip. Cut a length of card the circumference of your plant pot. Attach a length of double-sided tape to one side of the card. Press the stitched band on to the tape, keeping the design central. Turn the stitching over, so that the card is facing up. Attach double-sided tape to the cardboard, then fold the excess linen over on to the tape. Use double-sided tape to attach the stitching to the top of the plant pot.

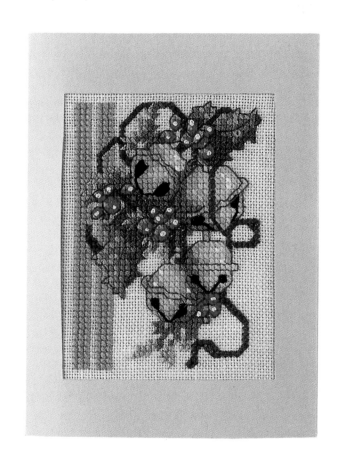

Jolly Santa Stocking

This bright, cheerful Santa stocking is sure to become a much loved part of your Christmas festivities. Santa's happy face and cute button nose will put a smile on the face of children young and old

- ❧ *Cream Zweigart Belfast linen, 32 count – 11.5x38cm (4½x15in)*
- ❧ *DMC stranded cotton (floss) in the colours listed in the key*
- ❧ *Red fur fabric 11.5x38cm (4½x15in)*
- ❧ *White fur fabric 35.5x15cm (14x6in); one 10cm (4in) circle*
- ❧ *Red pajama cord 12.5cm (5in)*
- ❧ *Tapestry needle No 24*
- ❧ *Large eyed needle*
- ❧ *White sewing thread and needle*
- ❧ *White tacking thread*

1 Mark the centre of your linen and oversew around the edges to prevent fraying. Work Santa from the centre out following the chart and key on pages 94 and 95. Use five strands of stranded cotton (floss) for the cross stitch and two strands for the backstitch, working each stitch on the chart over four threads of fabric. Wash and press the stitched linen following the instructions on page 108.

2 Carefully cut around the stitched Santa shape, leaving 1cm (⅜in) of blank fabric around the edges of the design. Lay the stitched stocking shape on the reverse side of the red fur fabric. Draw around the shape, transferring it to the fur fabric.

3 With right sides together, pin then tack the stitched stocking shape to the fur fabric following the outline of the design, and rounding off any sharp corners at the heel and toe. Neaten the seam then clip the seam allowance on the curves.

4 Still working on the wrong side of the stocking, cut a piece of white fur fabric 15cm (6in) wide and long enough to fit around the top of the stocking, adding 2cm (¾in) for the seam allowance.

5 To make the fur cuff, join the short edges of the white fur fabric together with a 1cm (⅜in) seam allowance. With right sides together, and working on the wrong side of the stitching, join the cuff to the top of the stocking along the top edge of the design. Fold half the cuff over to meet the inside of the stocking. Still working on the wrong side, catch stitch the cuff to the inside of the stocking. Turn the stocking to the right side.

6 To make the bobble, cut a 10cm (4in) circle of white fur fabric, and make a row of large running stitches around the edge. Place a small amount of stuffing in the middle of the fur circle then pull up the running stitches to make a bobble. Thread a large eyed needle with red pajama cord, tie a knot in one end and then make a stitch into the top of the bobble. With the bobble attached to the cord, push the needle through to the inside of the stocking, just below the cuff on the back seam. Remove the needle from the cord. Adjust the length of the cord on the outside of the stocking, so that the bobble hangs just below the cuff. Tie the cord end inside the stocking in a knot, to hold it in place.

This jolly Santa stocking can be hung up by the fireplace on Christmas Eve, so that when Santa calls he can have a special place to leave treats and small gifts.

Winter Sampler

DMC stranded cotton (floss)

·	Blanc
■	310
▨	311
▽	322
↑	415
✕	434
O	436
+	738
▬	898
<	931
U	986
=	989
→	3752

Blended cross stitch

H	Blanc + **
S	813 + *
L	828 + *

Backstitch

╱	310
╱	311
╱	322
╱	434
╱	898
╱	986

French knots

●	434

For blended cross stitch
add Kreinek blending
filament to the stranded
cotton (floss) colours
shown in the key.

** = 2 strands of 100HL

* = 1 strand of 014

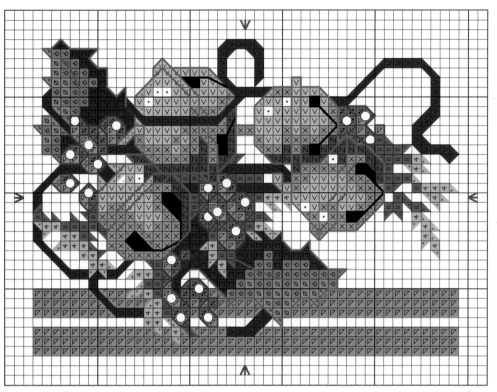

Christmas
Cards

Repeat Border

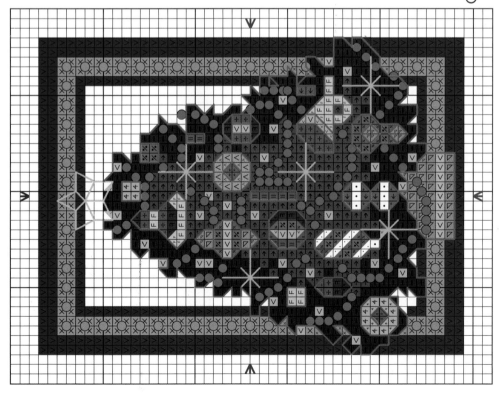

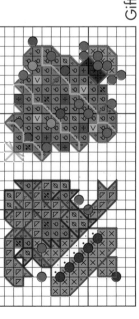

Gift Tags

Christmas Tree Decorations

DMC stranded cotton (floss)

	Blanc															948
·	Blanc														○	948
■	310														✦	954
⅜	321														■	3345
	367														↑	3347
H	472														◨	3688
C	552														←	3774
+	553													
+	554										**Backstitch**
↓	720										◿	310
◁	722										◿	321
∨	725										◿	725
⋈	727										◿	780
▷	761										◿	801
N	780										◿	814
✕	783										◿	826
	801										◿	3345
	814										◿	3685
	815										**French knots**
F	825										◖	Blanc
M	826										●	321
◔	827										●	433
∅	904										●	725
▣	906										●	553
=	907										●	780
◿	911										●	907
	945										●	995

Musical Decoration

Santa Decoration

Pear Tree Decoration

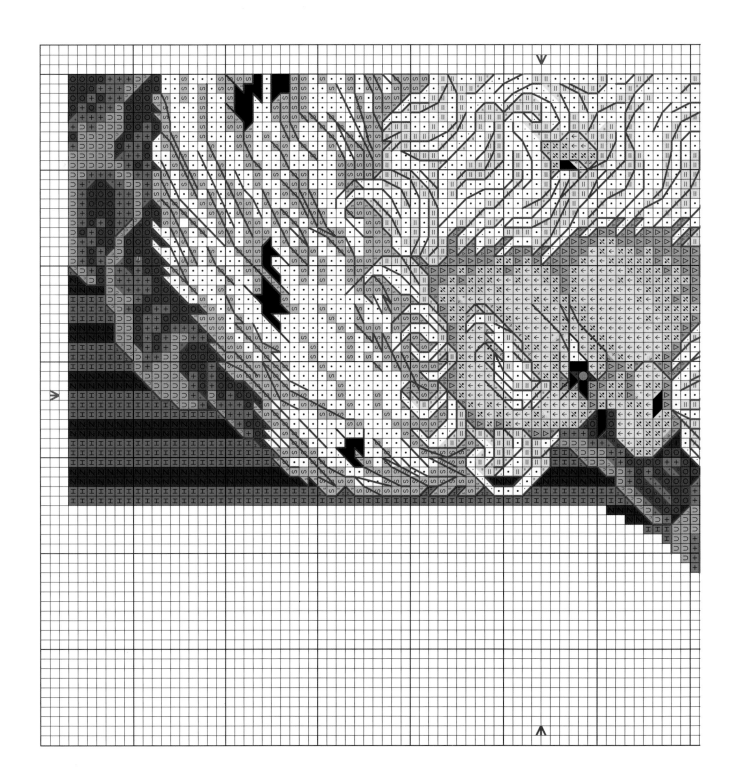

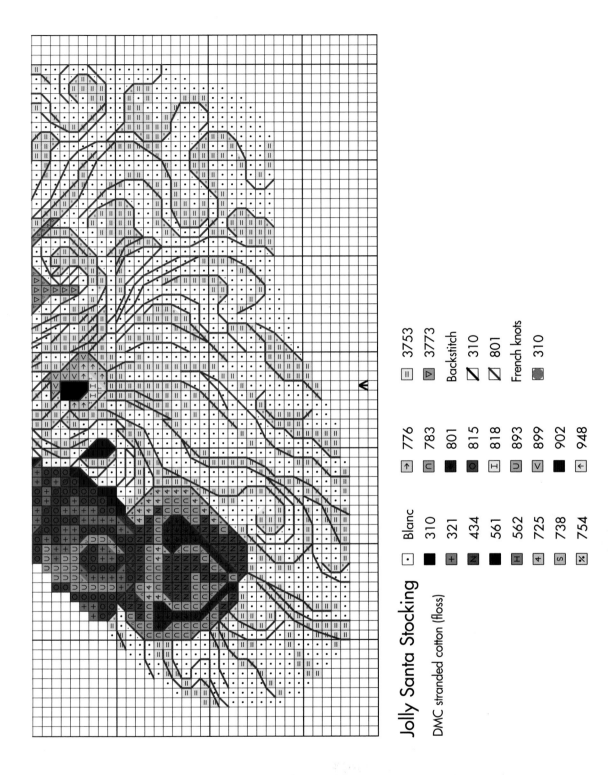

Jolly Santa Stocking

DMC stranded cotton (floss)

·	Blanc	↑	776	⊞	3753
■	310	⊂	783	▷	3773
+	321	■	801		Backstitch
Z	434	⊙	815	◪	310
■	561	⊞	818	◪	801
H	562	⊔	893		French knots
+	725	V	899	▦	310
s	738	■	902		
⊠	754	←	948		

Snow and Santa
DMC stranded cotton (floss)

	Xst	BS	FK
Blanc	·		
321	↑		
326	▽		
335	%		
434	S	/	
699	+		
739	<		
783	O		
801	→	/	◼
932	I	/	
945	∩		
957	Z		
986	H	/	
988	N		
3024		/	
3753	‖		
3761	✕		
3765		/	◼
3773	↓		
3774	4		
Gold*		/	

*Metallic thread

Snow

Santa

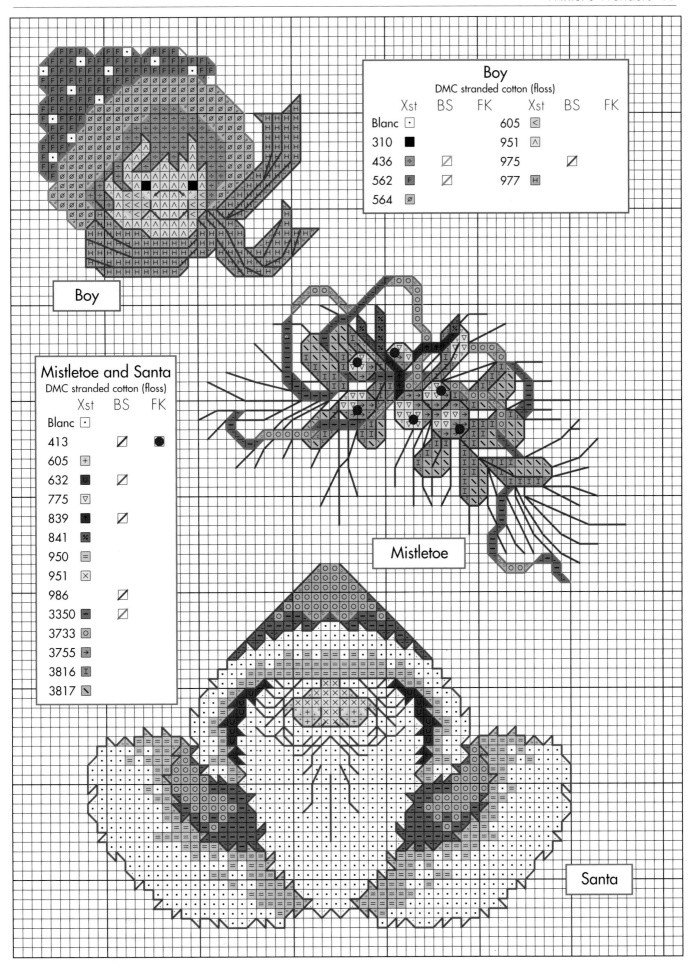

Boy

Boy
DMC stranded cotton (floss)

	Xst	BS	FK		Xst	BS	FK
Blanc	·			605	<		
310	■			951	∧		
436	+	/		975		/	
562	F	/		977	H		
564	⊘						

Mistletoe and Santa
DMC stranded cotton (floss)

	Xst	BS	FK
Blanc	·		
413		/	●
605	+		
632	U	/	
775	▽		
839	✳	/	
841	▨		
950	=		
951	✕		
986		/	
3350	−	/	
3733	O		
3755	→		
3816	I		
3817	◨		

Mistletoe

Santa

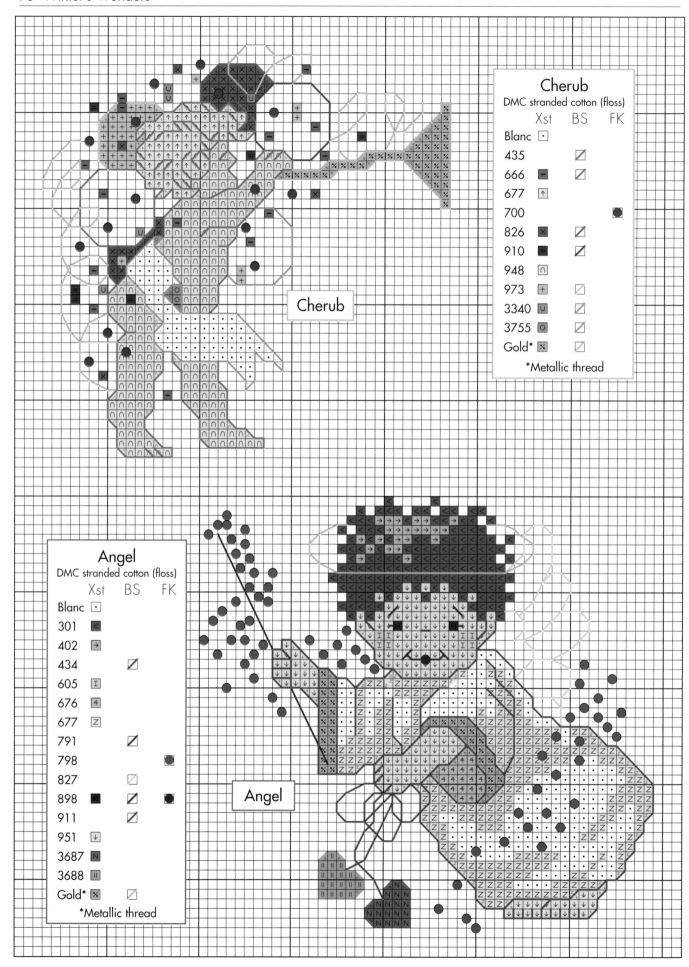

Cherub
DMC stranded cotton (floss)

	Xst	BS	FK
Blanc	·		
435		⊘	
666	−	⊘	
677	↑		
700			⬤
826	✕	⊘	
910	⊞	⊘	
948	∩		
973	+	⊘	
3340	U	⊘	
3755	○	⊘	
Gold*	⅔	⊘	

*Metallic thread

Cherub

Angel
DMC stranded cotton (floss)

	Xst	BS	FK
Blanc	·		
301	◄		
402	→		
434		⊘	
605	I		
676	4		
677	Z		
791		⊘	
798			⬤
827		⊘	
898	⊞	⊘	⬤
911		⊘	
951	↓		
3687	N		
3688	‖		
Gold*	⅔	⊘	

*Metallic thread

Angel

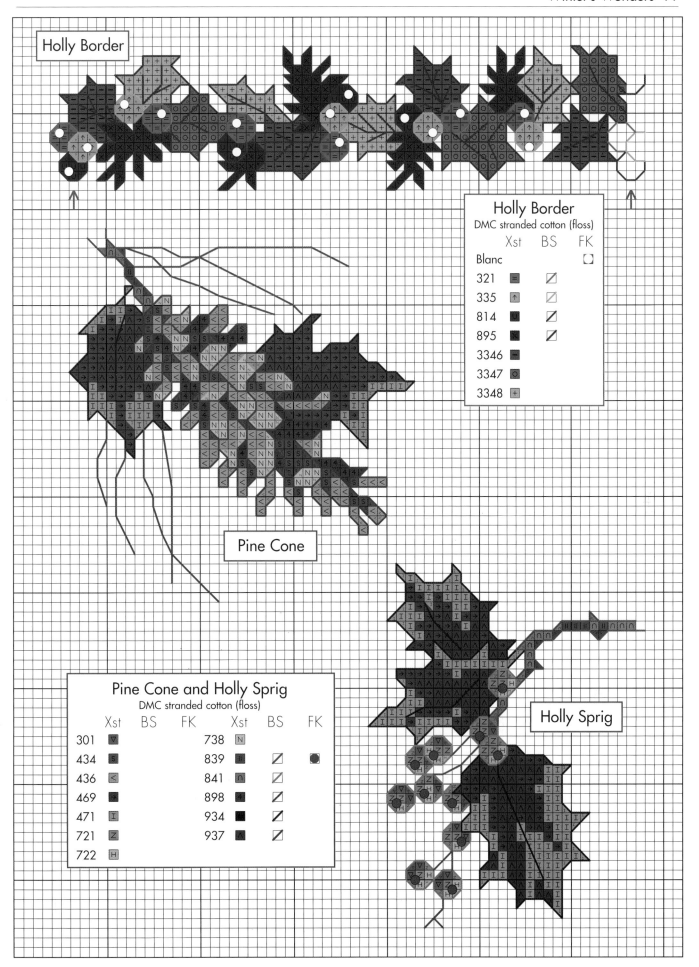

Holly Border

Holly Border
DMC stranded cotton (floss)

	Xst	BS	FK
Blanc			◌
321	=	◪	
335	↑	◪	
814	■	◪	
895	■	◪	
3346	▬		
3347	◉		
3348	+		

Pine Cone

Holly Sprig

Pine Cone and Holly Sprig
DMC stranded cotton (floss)

	Xst	BS	FK		Xst	BS	FK
301	▽			738	N		
434	S			839	⫼	◪	◼
436	<			841	∩	◪	
469	➤			898	✚	◪	
471	I			934	■	◪	
721	Z			937	∧	◪	
722	H						

Reindeer

Sleigh

Reindeer and Sleigh
DMC stranded cotton (floss)

	Xst	BS	FK
Blanc	·	◪	
312	■	◪	
814	▬		
Gold*	◉	◪	◉

*Metallic thread

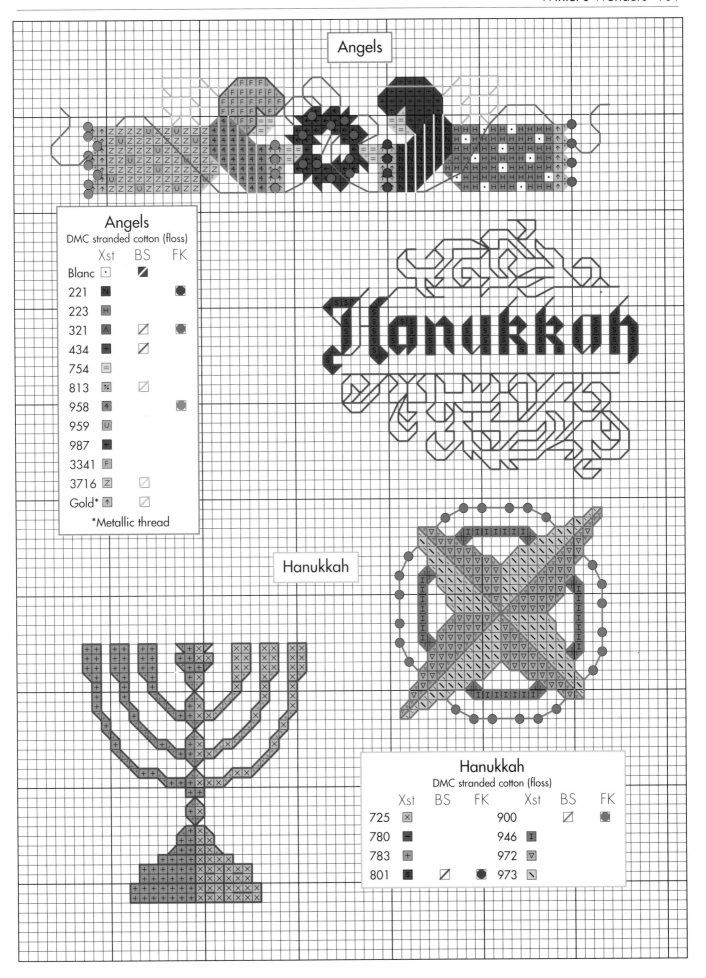

Angels

Angels
DMC stranded cotton (floss)

	Xst	BS	FK
Blanc	·	◩	
221	N		●
223	H		
321	∧	◿	●
434	⊞	◿	
754	=		
813	▨	◿	
958	4		●
959	U		
987	◄		
3341	F		
3716	Z	◿	
Gold*	↑	◿	

*Metallic thread

Hanukkah

Hanukkah
DMC stranded cotton (floss)

	Xst	BS	FK		Xst	BS	FK
725	⊠			900		◿	●
780	▬			946	I		
783	+			972	▽		
801	S	◿	●	973	◺		

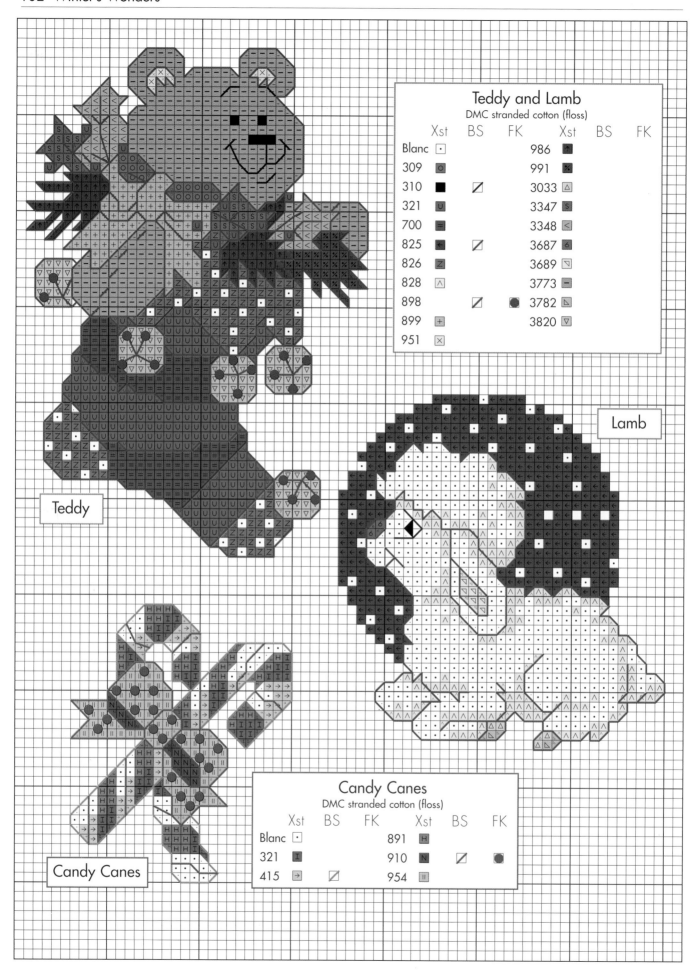

Teddy and Lamb
DMC stranded cotton (floss)

	Xst	BS	FK		Xst	BS	FK
Blanc	·			986	↑		
309	○			991	✖		
310	■	◰		3033	△		
321	U			3347	S		
700	═			3348	<		
825	◪	◰		3687	◿		
826	Z			3689	◺		
828	∧			3773	─		
898		◰	●	3782	◹		
899	+			3820	▽		
951	✕						

Teddy

Lamb

Candy Canes
DMC stranded cotton (floss)

	Xst	BS	FK		Xst	BS	FK
Blanc	·			891	H		
321	▮			910	N	◰	●
415	→	◰		954	▯		

Candy Canes

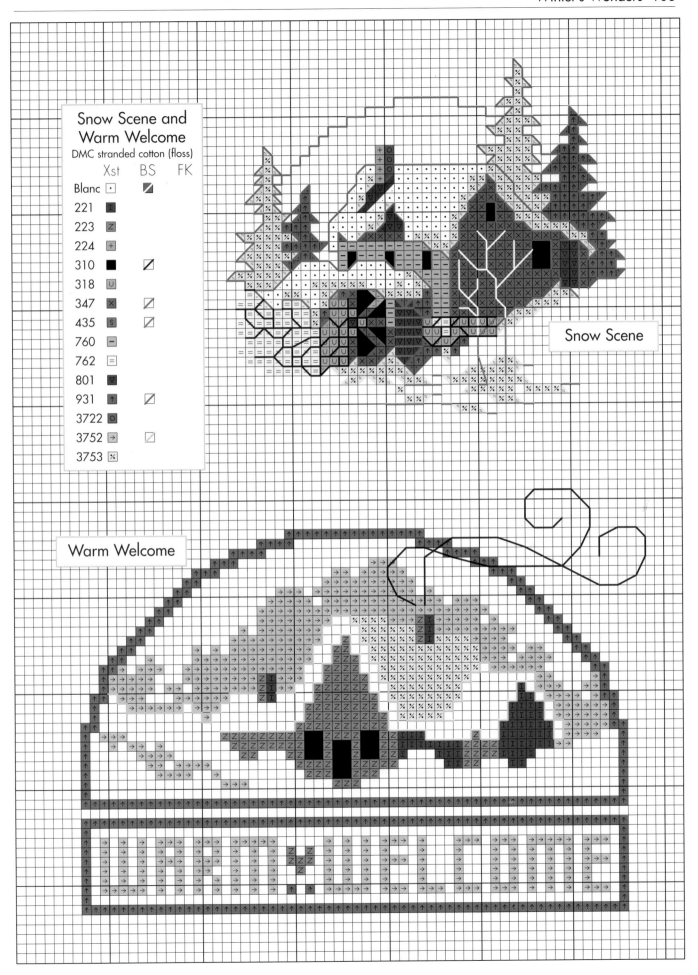

Snow Scene and
Warm Welcome
DMC stranded cotton (floss)

	Xst	BS	FK
Blanc	⊡	◹	
221	▣		
223	☒		
224	➕		
310	■	◹	
318	Ц		
347	☒	◹	
435	⒮	◹	
760	▬		
762	▤		
801	▽		
931	↑	◹	
3722	⊙		
3752	→	◹	
3753	⊠		

Snow Scene

Warm Welcome

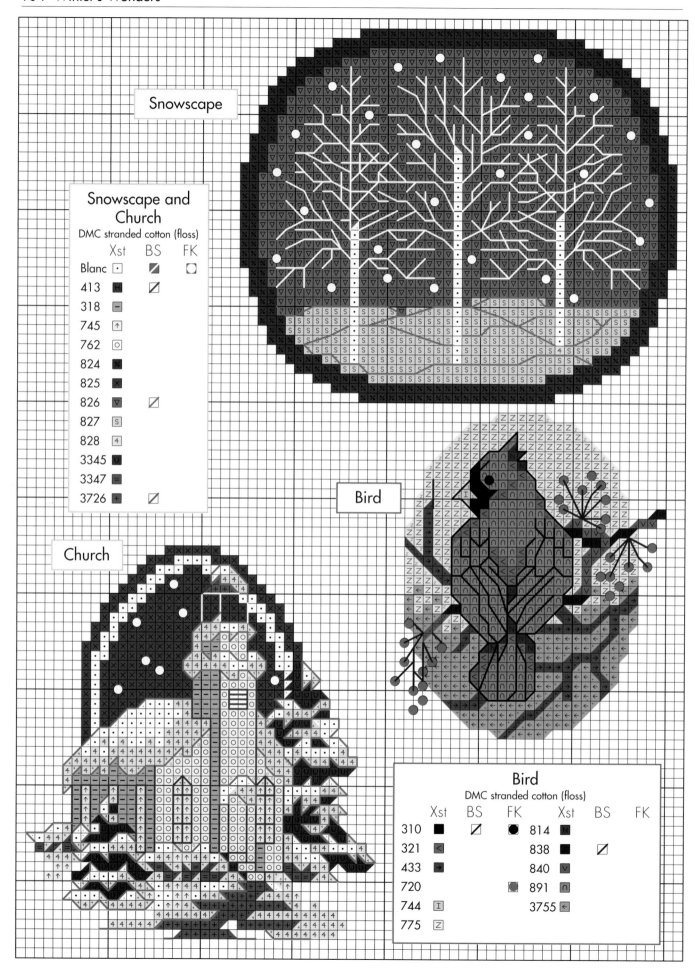

Snowscape

Snowscape and Church
DMC stranded cotton (floss)

	Xst	BS	FK
Blanc	·	▨	◡
413	▨	▨	
318	−		
745	↑		
762	○		
824	▨		
825	✕		
826	▽	▨	
827	S		
828	4		
3345	∪		
3347	▬		
3726	✚	▨	

Bird

Church

Bird
DMC stranded cotton (floss)

	Xst	BS	FK		Xst	BS	FK
310	■	▨	●	814	▨		
321	◂			838	■	▨	
433	▸			840	∨		
720				891	∩		
744	I			3755	◂		
775	Z						

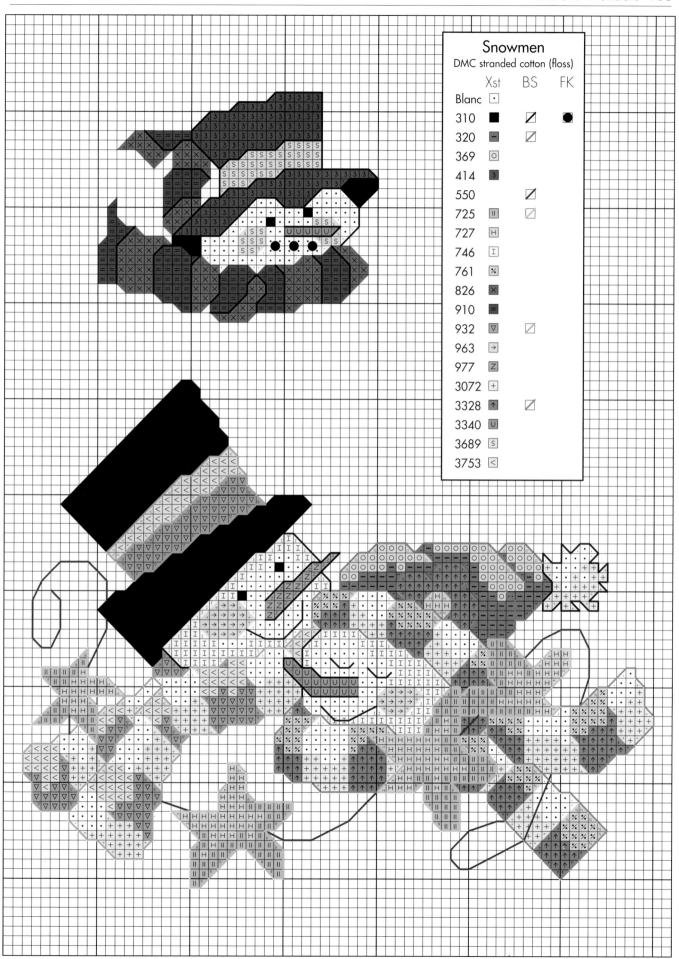

Snowmen
DMC stranded cotton (floss)

	Xst	BS	FK
Blanc	·		
310	■	◸	●
320	−	◸	
369	○		
414	3		
550		◸	
725	‖	◸	
727	H		
746	I		
761	٪		
826	✕		
910	▬		
932	▽	◸	
963	→		
977	Z		
3072	+		
3328	↑	◸	
3340	U		
3689	s		
3753	<		

Alphabet Library

Use this alphabet to personalise the note block, folder and ruler, which can be found in the Autumnal Desk Set project starting on page 62.

Templates

Use the templates on this page to create the summer t-shirt motif on page 38, autumnal gift tags on page 63, and the Christmas tree decorations on page 83 and 86.

Autumnal Gift Tag – page 63

Pear Tree Decoration – page 86

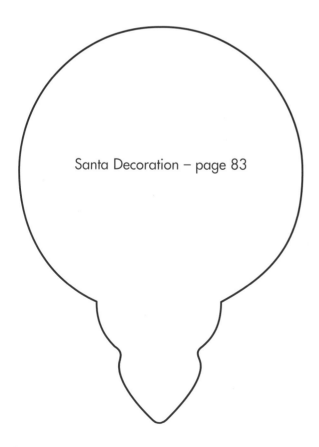

Santa Decoration – page 83

Dolphin Motif – page 38

Essential Techniques

Starting and Finishing

To start off your first length of thread, make a knot at one end and push the needle through to the back of the fabric, about 3cm (1¼in) from your starting point, leaving the knot on the right side. Stitch towards the knot, securing the thread at the back of the fabric as you go. When the thread is secure, cut off the knot.

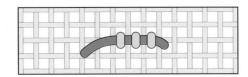

To finish off a thread or start new threads, simply weave the thread into the back of several worked stitches and then trim off neatly.

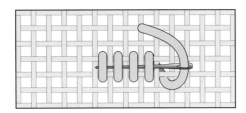

Cross Stitch

Each coloured square on the chart represents one cross on the evenweave fabric. If the fabric is linen each stitch would be worked over two threads of fabric. A cross stitch is worked in two stages: a diagonal stitch is worked over one block of fabric (Aida), or two threads (finer fabric like linen) from the bottom left of the stitch to the top right. The second part of the stitch is worked in the opposite direction to form a cross.

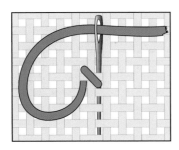

Backstitch and Outlining

Backstitch is indicated on the charts by a solid coloured line. It is worked on its own, on top of stitches for detail, or as an outline around areas of cross stitch to give definition.

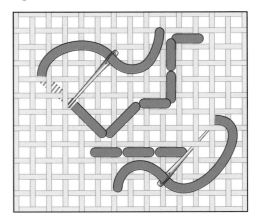

Blanket Stitch

This stitch is used to edge fabric to stop it fraying and for decoration. Bring the needle out on the lower line shown in the diagram below. Re-insert the needle at 1 on the upper line and out again at 2, keeping the thread under the needle point so a loop is formed.

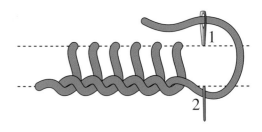

Couching Stitch

Couching stitch is a way of attaching a length of thread to the surface of the fabric, without stitching through the thread. It is easier to lay the thread to be couched on a line marked on the fabric – this may be a seam line, a fabric grain line, or a line marked with pen. Lay the thread to be couched on the fabric, holding it firmly in place with your finger. Bring the needle out exactly on the couching line and then make

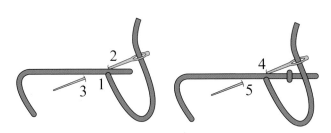

a very small stitch over the couching thread and back into the fabric at the point where the needle first emerged. Take the needle along the back of the fabric and come out on the couching line, a short distance from the first stitch. Make another small stitch over the thread, and back into the fabric. Continue in this way, following the line with the couching thread and keeping the stitches evenly spaced. To finish off, take the needle to the back of the fabric and weave it through the back of a few worked stitches.

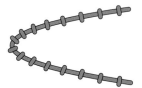

Quilting Stitch

To quilt the fabric layers together, make a row of small neat running stitches through all the layers of fabric, passing the thread under and over the fabric with regular spacing.

Washing and Ironing Cross Stitch

Handling even the smallest piece of cross stitch can make the threads look flat and dull, so always wash your work before it is framed or mounted. Swish your stitching in luke warm water and, if the colours bleed, rinse with fresh water until the water is clear. Do not be tempted to stop rinsing unless you are absolutely sure the bleeding has stopped. Roll your stitching up in a clean towel and squeeze gently to remove most of the water. On a second, fluffy towel, place your design face down, cover with a clean cloth and iron until the stitching is dry.

Mounting and Framing

It is best to take large cross stitch designs to a professional framer who will advise you on displaying your work. If you would prefer to lace your own work then most framers will be happy to make the frame and cut the mount and backboard for you. If you are mounting the work yourself use acid-free board in a pale colour. The mount board should be cut to fit inside your picture frame, allowing for the thickness of material that will be wrapped over the board. There are two methods of attaching the stitching to the board – taping and lacing.

Taping

Place the cut board on the reverse side of your stitching. Starting from the centre of one of the longest sides, fold the excess fabric over on to the board, then pin through the fabric and into the edge of the board. Repeat along all four sides of the board. Use strips of double-sided tape to hold the fabric on to the back of the board. Remove the pins once the work is secured.

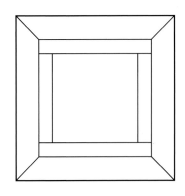

Lacing

Pin the work along the edges of the board in the same way as for the taping. Working from the centre of one side, and using very long lengths of strong thread begin lacing backwards and forwards across the gap between the fabric overlap, while keeping the fabric on the right side stretched. Remove the pins. Repeat for the other two sides, taking care to mitre the corners or turn the corners in neatly.

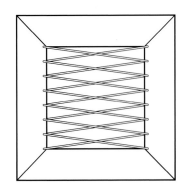

Acknowledgements

The publishers would like to thank the following people:
Jo Strowger, Barbara Phillips, Christine Thompson, Michaela Learner and
Doreen Holland for their expert stitching;
John Gollop for his excellent photography; and Susan and Martin Penny for editing and
designing the book, and preparing the charts.

Suppliers

When writing to any of the companies listed below, please include a stamped addressed
envelope for your reply.

Framecraft
372-376 Summer Lane, Hockley, Birmingham,
B19 3QA
*Mill Hill beads, luggage tag, Sudberry tray, note
block and ruler.*

DMC Creative World Ltd
Pullman Road, Wigston, Leicester LE8 2DY
Zweigart Aida, linen and stranded cotton.

Coats Crafts Ltd
PO Box 22, The Lingfield Estate, McMullen Road,
Darlington, Co Durham DL1 1YQ
Balger blending filament.

Craft Creations Ltd
2C Ingersoll House, Dalamare Road, Cheshunt,
Herts EN8 9ND
Greetings card blanks.

The DMC Corporation
Port Kearney Bld, 10 South Kearney,
NJ 070732-0650, USA
Zweigart Aida, linen and stranded cotton.

Gay Bowles Sales Inc
PO Box 1060, Janesville, WI, USA

Anne Brinkley Designs Inc
761 Palmer Avenue, Holmdel, NJ 97733, USA

Ireland Needlecraft Pty Ltd
2-4 Keppel Drive, Hallam, Victoria 3803, Australia

DMC Needlecraft Pty
PO Box 317, Earlswood 2206, New South Wales
2204, Australia
Zweigart Aida, linen and stranded cotton.

Chart Subject Index

Index

Entries in *italics* indicate illustrations, **bold** indicates charts.